THE BATTLE OF EL ALAMEIN

THE BATTLE OF EL ALAMEIN

Fortress in the Sand

FRED MAJDALANY

UNIVERSITY OF PENNSYLVANIA PRESS

Philadelphia

Originally published 1965 by J.B. Lippincott Company
Copyright © 1965 Fred Majdalany

Printed in the United States of America on acid-free paper

10 9 8 7 6 5 4 3 2 1

Published 2003 by
University of Pennsylvania Press
Philadelphia, Pennsylvania 19104-4011

Library of Congress Cataloging-in-Publication Data

Majdalany, F. (Fred), 1913–
    The battle of El Alamein : fortress in the sand / Fred Majdalany.
        p. cm.
    Originally published: Philadelphia : Lippincott, 1965.
    Includes bibliographical references and index.
    ISBN 0-8122-1850-7 (paper : alk. paper)
    1. El Alamein, Battle of, Egypt, 1942. I. Title.
D766.9 .M3   2003
940.54'23—dc21   2002072881

CONTENTS

MAPS

PREFACE

I am indebted to Captain B. H. Liddell Hart for documentary material which he kindly placed at my disposal; to Dr. Brian Bond, Lecturer in History at Liverpool University, who read the manuscript and was able to draw my attention to some factual slips; to Mr. Hanson W. Baldwin, Military Editor of the New York *Times*, for a number of valuable editorial suggestions; and to the ever-helpful Mr. D. W. King, O.B.E., of the War Department Library.

F. M.

Little Saling, Essex.
September 1964

THE BATTLE OF EL ALAMEIN

A PRIVATE WAR

1 THE STRATEGY of the Second World War gave rise, in its diffuse worldwide implication to a number of campaigns so distinctive in character and locality that they seemed to aspire to an existence of their own outside the mainstream of the war. Of these private wars, as one may think of them, none was more self-contained and even esoteric than the campaign which the nations of the British Commonwealth fought against the German-Italian alliance in the Western Desert of Egypt and Libya between the autumns of 1940 and 1942.

In time it spanned the critical period of Britain's fighting recovery from near-defeat and seemingly forlorn resistance without allies to the unmistakable turning point that placed the feasibility of ultimate victory beyond doubt. It was this timing that above all gave the desert campaign its special significance in the British war context of 1939–45. It is indicative of the interlocking vagaries of modern global strategy that this battle of a nation for survival should have been fought, by her main land force at that time in the field, three thousand miles from the mother country, in the empty desert of North Africa.

But if its timing gave the campaign in the desert its historic significance, what gave to it its special nature and its mystique—for it was no less than that—was the ground over which it was fought; ground, the raw material of the soldier, always in the end gives a battle or a campaign its persona and its uniqueness.

Some account of this battleground and the campaign as a whole must be given if we are to re-create, in its moral and psychological as well as its historical and purely military perspective, the battle which brought the campaign to its grand climax, the second battle of El Alamein.

When, in the summer of 1940, the fall of France completed Hitler's conquest of Europe and the British people prepared in pugnacious impotence to fight the invasion of their shores that then seemed inevitable, the defense of the United Kingdom itself was scarcely more important to Britain than the defense of Egypt. Not only because of the Suez Canal, the vital Egyptian link in the imperial lifeline to India and Australasia, but also because of oil. Egypt was militarily the key to the vast Middle East on which Britain was almost entirely dependent for oil, and the mechanization of armies between the two world wars had made oil as important as ammunition. An army no longer marched on its stomach but on its gasoline tanks. Quite simply, defeat in the Middle East could knock Britain out of the war in a matter of weeks.[1]*

With this bleak consideration in the forefront of her strategic thinking, Britain had long-standing agreements with Egypt under which British naval, military and air forces were permanently stationed in that country. These bases included the great port of Alexandria, which—with Gibraltar and Malta —completed a trio of naval bastions that gave the Royal Navy command of the Mediterranean. Although a subsequent generation of Egyptian rulers would repudiate these arrangements

* Superior figures refer to Notes at end of text.

as disguised imperialism, Egypt's rulers at the time were grateful for the money as well as for the military protection that went with the deal. They were not unmindful that Mussolini's addition of Abyssinia to an Italian African empire already established in Libya was something that affected Egypt too.

When Hitler's victory in the west emboldened his weaker partner Mussolini to bring Italy into the war, Britain had two divisions in Egypt to pit against an Italian army of 215,000 in Cyrenaica and another 200,000 in Abyssinia, Eritrea and Somaliland to the south.[2]

That was in June, as Winston Churchill issued his rallying calls to resistance, and the tired soldiers from Dunkirk, along with the fresh soldiers who were daily being added to their number, stood to arms around the British coastline watching for the German invasion fleets. In August and September Hitler's invasion was frustrated by the fighter pilots of the Royal Air Force who, in the Battle of Britain, prevented the *Luftwaffe* from gaining the vital air superiority that was the essential preliminary. When it became clear that the invasion was off, at least until the following spring, it began to look as though the British Army's next battles would be fought, a little incredibly as far as the ordinary Briton was concerned, at the threshold of Egypt. For this was where the threat to Britain's Middle East oil would come. Britain's latest generation of young fighting men would fight not in the Maginot Line, as they had expected to do; not in Flanders, like their fathers; not in the pillboxes and bunkers that had hurriedly been thrown up on the coast of their native land—but in the hot, waterless western approach to, of all places, Egypt . . . and against Italians. This was not the picture of war on which they had been brought up by their fathers. Nor was it the picture painted by books and films of the 1914–18 war.

The Western Desert is a torrid wasteland extending from the Mediterranean to the Sahara and taking in most of Egypt and Libya. But for practical purposes that part of it in which the campaign of 1940–42 was fought may be defined as a stretch of 500 miles embracing the western two-thirds of Egypt and the eastern half of Libya, the then Italian colony of Cyrenaica.

This was not so much an area as a field of play, 700 miles

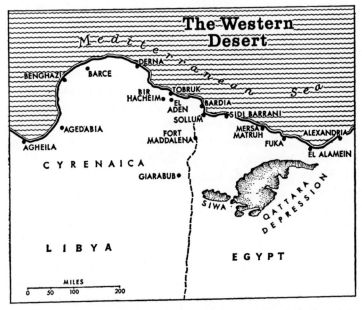

long, with Alexandria and Benghazi as the goals between which the tide of war commuted in rapid advance and retreat, favoring first one side, then the other. The width of the field was whatever the opposing tank generals chose or had the supply capability to make it.

The Western Desert is a desolate scorching emptiness; not the golden sand dunes of romantic imagination, but ranging in color from dun to grit gray, and near the coast, because of a limestone base, a dazzling white that in the heat of midday is almost incandescent. There is no vegetation except for patches and tufts of stringy camel scrub; no living creatures other than scorpions, little horned vipers, and a few other reptiles and rodents including the desert rat. There are myriads of tiny snails and even more myriads of flies, one of the two great scourges of the desert soldiers. Occasionally a gazelle might be glimpsed, or a few Bedouin proceeding, as is their mysterious way, from nowhere to nowhere.

On the coast it rains a few times a year, but inland there may be no rain for years. Water, therefore, can be found only by boring, and every drop the fighting man needs must be carried to him—an additional strain on the supply services which, in this kind of warfare, are already overburdened.

The first impression of the desert is that it is featureless and quite flat except for some low ridges and conspicuous high points of rock which stand out starkly in isolation in certain areas. Offsetting these ridges are a number of depressions of corresponding depth and an escarpment which is a feature of the whole area, extending along the coast of Cyrenaica and then, inside the Egyptian border, turning southeast.

However, this impression of infinite flatness which strikes the newcomer to the desert is deceptive. When the eye has become accustomed to "feeling" it with the sense of ground that a good soldier must cultivate until it is instinctive, the desert discloses barely discernible folds and undulations, sufficient to conceal the ungainly outline of a tank or gun or a group of men forming up to assault. Concealment may be abetted by swirling dust and sand or by the optical deception of excessive heat and light and the shimmering mirage they combine to create.

The going is firm over most of this northern plateau of the desert that accommodated the battles; having a basis of rock below its shallow carpet of sand, it is firm enough for tanks as well as wheeled vehicles. But care had to be taken to avoid the periodic expanses of soft sand in which vehicles could swiftly bog. At the same time the rock base that was good for the fighting vehicles was not so good for the fighting men, for normally they could not dig far into its crust without the aid of drills and explosives, and an infantryman deprived of the power to dig himself and his guns into cover is naked and defenseless.

If men have to fight wars there could be no more suitable place anywhere in which to do so than this hard-based northern plateau of the Western Desert: an empty nothingness large enough and mostly firm enough to exercise a million tanks and trucks and guns if one had them; a boundless void in which all the infernal engines and explosive frightfulness of modern war could be deployed without people, animals, buildings or cultivated lands to get in the way. There was absolutely no one and nothing to damage except the men and equipment of the opposing army.

The outstanding built-in advantage of this place as a battleground was the freedom it afforded for tactical maneuver. But battlegrounds, like men, have the defects of their virtues. This freedom of maneuver that was the desert's precious gift to those who came to fight created a compensating problem of supply.

It was one thing to deploy free-ranging tanks by the hundred; another to keep them supplied with enough fuel to keep them fighting; and not fuel only, but everything else that a fighting army needs. In the desert this meant not only fuel, ammunition and food, but water. This became the key to the desert fighting: to achieve a balance between the quite abnormal power of movement for tactical advantage and the limitation it imposed on the capacity to keep equipment viable and supplied. This had the paradoxical effect that as an all-mechanized army advanced rapidly in victory and its bases receded far to the rear it was bound to become weaker as it outran its ability to support itself. Especially in fuel (for the thirst of an armored division is prodigious); while the other side, retreating just as fast but toward, instead of away from, its bases, became correspondingly stronger as its successful opponent became weaker.

The problem of supply, with the special implications peculiar to the desert, overshadowed all else in this campaign which seemed at times like a cross between a sporting contest and a military training exercise with live ammunition.

That was the practical basis of the desert war. There were other aspects that printed their quality indelibly on the minds and memories of those who came to fight. There was the sense of emptiness which at first all men found oppressive, some positively frightening; a sort of extended agoraphobia; a fear of being sucked into the unholy emptiness and being lost forever.

This fear of becoming lost was well-founded. In so featureless a void it was desperately easy to lose oneself. Each of the armies that came to the desert to fight built up its own folklore of stories of men getting lost. A compass was essential for the simplest journey. A British general learned this the hard way on his first night in the desert when it took him two hours to reach the Officers' Mess from his dugout 400 yards away.

But even more than the emptiness, even more than the inescapable flies, there was something else. Every battlefield has its quintessential obsessive torment: the one by which it is remembered in perpetuity by those who fought it. In earlier wars it had been mud. In the Western Desert it was dust—inundating, permeating, ubiquitous dust stirred up by many machines and driven by merciless hot air currents. "And always," wrote Alexander Clifford, the war correspondent, "there was the dust—dust as fine as snuff or flour which can seep through closed lips and eyelids, through any clothing;

which gets into food and gun barrels and aeroplane engines; which, when it blows, makes men pray for deliverance."[3]

This, then, was where, in the summer of 1940, a British garrison of 55,000 (including, of course, base troops of all kinds) braced themselves to defend Egypt and Britain's oil against Italian forces five times as numerous under the command of Marshal Rodolfo Graziani. Luckily for the British, Graziani showed little disposition to be aggressive. Not until the middle of September did he move cautiously across the Egyptian frontier (a meaningless dividing line marked only by 400 miles of barbed wire erected, quite uselessly, by the Italians). Count Galeazzo Ciano, Italy's Foreign Minister, noted: "Never has a military operation been undertaken so much against the will of the commanders."[4] General Sir Archibald (later Field-Marshal Earl) Wavell, Commander-in-Chief in the Middle East, saw a chance to put into practice the ancient adage that attack is the best form of defense. Accordingly, in December, the Western Desert Force—comprising no more than one infantry and one armored division and a handful of additional tanks—launched under General Sir Richard O'Connor a David and Goliath offensive near Sidi Barrani which in ten brilliant weeks took it 500 miles to Benghazi, destroying in the process ten Italian divisions, capturing 130,000 prisoners, 400 tanks and 1,290 guns at a cost of under 2,000 killed, wounded and missing.[5] The capture of the airfields of Cyrenaica, invaluable as a base from which to support Malta, offset the activity of the Italian navy, now a factor to be reckoned with in the new power setup in the Mediterranean.

It was a fantastic and slightly unbelievable victory at a time when the British public and the British Army badly needed one. The notion that the Royal Navy and Royal Air Force were fighting the war without any help from the British Army had become a little more than a joke. The "miracle" of Dunkirk was by now being seen realistically for what it was: a

disaster; and earlier there had been Norway. Could the Army
do anything right? Even the poor civilians had now had their
first taste of bombing. A victory at last for the British Army
was more than welcome.

In February 1941 there seemed to be nothing to stop Gen.
O'Connor and his victorious little Western Desert Force from
continuing their blitzkrieg into Tripolitania and on to Tripoli.
But unhappily General Wavell was now ordered to divert some
of his forces to help defend Greece and Crete—a well-meaning
gesture by the British Cabinet which was to lead, however, to
two more withdrawals by British forces leaving behind equipment that could ill be spared. Weakened for the time being
by the diversion to Greece, Western Desert Force had no
alternative but to pass to the defensive on ground it well knew
to be unsuited to the purpose.

It was now that the German High Command decided that
it had better do something to help its Italian friends if Wavell's
army was not to go right on through Tripolitania and join up
with the French Colonial forces in Algeria and Tunisia—many
of whom would be glad to renounce the Vichy regime. A
small mobile German force was hurriedly sent to Tripoli—a
nucleus that would later become the 21st Panzer Division and
then, with the 15th Panzer Division, would make up the German Afrika Korps. In command of this embryonic force was
General Erwin Rommel, a tough tank general who had done
well in France in command of a panzer division.

A new dynamic force had thus come into the desert picture, a leader with a gift for inspiring devotion in those he
commanded, nearly equaled at times by the admiration of his
opponents. One of the star personalities of the war had stepped
on to the stage.

The Germans had not meant to become involved in Africa. General Siegfried Westphal, who for a time was Rommel's chief of staff, has recounted how, when maps of all pos-

sible potential theaters of war were being methodically prepared by the German General Staff, he himself gave instructions that North Africa need not be included—a decision with which his superiors concurred.[6] Nor, to begin with, did Mussolini want any German soldiers in Libya, a region in which he was jealously conscious of his own proprietorial responsibilities. It was not until total Italian defeat in Tripolitania seemed a real possibility as a result of the Wavell–O'Connor offensive that Rome itself appealed for German help.

The small German force which was sent to Tripoli in consequence—the force that would grow into the celebrated armored Afrika Korps of 15th and 21st Panzer Divisions, the spearhead of the German-Italian Panzerarmee Afrika—was sent rather grudgingly to please the Italians. It was given strictly limited aims.

Rommel was promised more forces, including the 15th Panzer Division, by the end of May, when his task would then be to destroy the British forces around Agedabia and possibly advance as far as Benghazi. The Italian High Command, under whom Rommel was placed, agreed with this plan—but it was much too cautious for Rommel himself. Against the wishes of both the German and Italian Command he decided, as Wavell had done in the previous autumn, that a swift unexpected blow may make up in surprise and speed for what it may lack in strength. On the last day of March he attacked the weakened British forces at El Agheila and Marsa el Brega, defeated them, and then, subordinating everything to speed, boldness and improvisation, he raced victoriously to the Egyptian frontier. Thus he recaptured in a few weeks all that the Italians had lost to the Western Desert Force. Except for Tobruk, which he invested and bypassed, and which was to hold out for many months sustained by the Royal Navy to the stage where troops could be brought in to relieve others that had been in the besieged port too long.

Rommel's swift reversal in the spring of the British winter victory knocked the gilt off two successes by British land forces elsewhere during the same early part of 1941. Two small armies of Commonwealth soldiers had converged on Abyssinia and Eritrea from the north and the south and taken another 185,000 Italian prisoners.

But when Rommel's turning of the tables in Libya was followed in due course by two more withdrawals of British troops—from Greece and Crete—the Army's stock was again low. "You can manage against the Italians," people said in effect, "but as soon as a few Germans appear on the scene we learn about yet another retreat." This was the kind of gibe commonly heard in Britain. It did little good to point out that Wavell's army had had to be emasculated just when it was ready to exploit its wonderful initial successes because the British Government chose to honor its obligation to help a hard-pressed Greek ally.

If one touches on this fluctuating prestige of the British Army and the feelings and moods engendered by the early disasters of the war, it is because they are an essential part of the story, and, as we shall see, highly relevant to the climactic battle that is the subject of this book. So many have forgotten, so many were too young to know or care, what the British people thought and felt about their army between 1940 and 1942; yet it is a vital aspect of what El Alamein was all about.

During the summer of 1941 Rommel made several unsuccessful attempts to capture Tobruk, and Wavell, under Cabinet pressure, began an abortive new offensive into Cyrenaica. General (later Field-Marshal) Sir Claude Auchinleck now took over from General Wavell as Commander-in-Chief and in November he launched a new offensive code-named CRU-SADER. Its three aims were the relief of Tobruk, the reconquest of Cyrenaica, and restoration of air and naval support for Malta by the recapture of the Cyrenaican airfields.

For the new offensive Western Desert Force had been greatly reinforced and renamed the Eighth Army. Its commander was Lieut.-General Sir Alan Cunningham. For the first time the British were to start an offensive with a superiority of tanks and aircraft.[7] Eighth Army had the equivalent of seven divisions against three German and seven Italian, but the British strength included 724 tanks against the enemy's 414, and the Desert Air Force had nearly 1,100 aircraft against the enemy's 320. The British offensive achieved its objectives—though not without heavy losses in men and tanks and a crisis of leadership at the climax of the battle that was resolved only by the resolute intervention of General Auchinleck himself, and resulting in the replacement of General Cunningham by Lieut.-General N. M. Ritchie.

By January the position was similar to what it had been a year before, the Axis army having pulled back as far as El Agheila on the Gulf of Sirte. Auchinleck, no matter to what extent his victory had been achieved by weight of numbers, had taught the Eighth Army that it could beat Rommel. But Auchinleck now had to release some of his forces for use on another front as his predecessor Wavell had had to do the year before: this time to the Far East, where Singapore fell early in February and the Japanese threat to Burma was developing. Two divisions, an armored brigade, and substantial air forces had to go east.

The melancholy history of the previous year now repeated itself in a third respect, a swift counterstroke by Gen. Rommel. This did not carry his army through to Egypt as in the previous year—Eighth Army managed to stop him on a line running south from El Gazala—but it meant that he had recaptured a sizable portion of the bulge of Cyrenaica, including the airfields that were so essential to the British if Malta was to be saved. It meant that Rommel now had a useful springboard for his next dash to Egypt; while Eighth Army was correspondingly farther away from the onward move into Tripolitania which Prime Minister Churchill was urging on Gen. Auchinleck. The effect was undoubtedly to diminish the hard-won victory of the Eighth Army at the turn of the year.

In early 1942 the two desert armies faced each other across Cyrenaica and prepared for the next phase of a contest in which the British had twice reached the opposite goal line, and the Axis once. Who would be ready first?

General Auchinleck was under greater pressure from home to reopen his offensive westwards. The Prime Minister was always impatient in the face of logistic reality as presented by his generals, and was apt to think that the generals were being much too cautious and unwilling to act until everything was "just right." On the other hand the generals had to face the military realities and the consequences, and the testimony of Field-Marshal Lord Alanbrooke and other distinguished soldiers makes it clear that behind the unquestioned and surpassing Churchill dynamic that inspired the British effort, especially in these early years of the long fight back from defeat, a distinct element of unreasonableness and even fantasy sometimes colored the Prime Minister's moods when he assumed the role of military strategist. Distance greatly aggravated the difficulties of this relationship between Middle East headquarters and London. But in General Auchinleck the Prime Minister was dealing with a first-class military brain allied to a rocklike character. Auchinleck was a man of integrity and courage who could not be stampeded.

Although a note of acrimony was not an uncommon feature of some of the cables from London to Cairo, Auchinleck's schedule of late May or early June as the earliest date a new offensive could be properly mounted was eventually agreed to in London. The Eighth Army under General Ritchie proceeded with a big buildup. This not only began with a thickening of minefields and other measures to make their firm base on the line south of Gazala firmer still, but included some elaborate measures like the extension of the railway and the water pipeline to the outskirts of Tobruk in support of their intended offensive.

On the other hand, Rommel was not under such intense pressure from his superiors. Rommel's problem was getting his superiors to take his supply problem seriously at all.

The German High Command . . . still failed to see the importance of the African theatre. They did not realise that with relatively small means, we could have won victories in the Near East which, in their strategic and economic value, would have far surpassed the conquest of the Don Bend. . . .

But it was not to be. Our demands for additional formations were refused on the grounds that with the huge demand for transport which the eastern front was making the creation of further motorised units for Africa was out of the question.

It was obvious that the High Command's opinion had not changed from that which they had expressed in 1941, namely, that Africa was a "lost cause."[8]

North Africa was still, in the German High Command's view, the most secondary of considerations. Rommel was in charge of nothing more important than a small task force sent to stiffen the Italian ally. If this recaptured Tobruk and forced the Eighth Army back across the Egyptian border for the second time that would be fine. The German High Command asked for no more. Let Rommel and the Italians get on with it. But Erwin Rommel was not temperamentally the kind of man to accept the idea of a supporting role in a subordinate campaign. He was a professional performer with a boundless belief in himself. By nature an opportunist and gambler with a taste for the calculated risk, he also was ineffably ambitious. Side shows might suit others, but for Rommel it had to be the big show or nothing. If necessary he would force his side show into the center of the stage. He had shown soon after his arrival in North Africa that it was possible to disobey orders and get away with it—provided it was done boldly and crowned with success, preferably dazzling success.

In April of 1942 Rommel's worry about his supplies was partly eased for him by Field-Marshal Albert Kesselring's air forces which had managed to regain temporary ascendancy over the central Mediterranean. Under this air cover ships carrying reinforcements and supplies of all kinds were able to evade the British Navy which earlier in the year had managed by its sinkings to reduce Rommel's monthly shipments to as little as 18,000 tons as compared with his estimated requirement of 60,000 tons each month.[9] Encouraged by his vastly improved supply situation and apprehensively aware of the scale on which the Eighth Army was preparing for its new effort which obviously would not be long delayed, Rommel decided that by making the most of his present air superiority, he could get his blow in first.

On the night of May 26, 1942, he struck with what was by this time the classic opening gambit of a desert offensive, the wide encircling sweep round the opponent's open southern flank, and intending to thrust directly northeast to Tobruk.

The tank strength of the respective forces again favored the Eighth Army which had 850 tanks to Rommel's 560—but 300 of the latter were the heaviest German tanks and had hitherto proved superior to anything used by the British.[10] This time, however, the British had up their sleeve 170 of a new tank, the American Grant, with a firepower that enabled Eighth Army's tank crews to challenge the German heavies for the first time on equal terms. In infantry the Eighth Army was also slightly superior with seven divisions to Rommel's six and a half.

Rommel personally led the attack at the head of his redoubtable Afrika Korps (15th and 21st Panzer Divisions) and the Ariete Division (the best of the Italian armored divisions).

The British Eighth Army welcomed the attack as an opportunity to put aside for the moment their own offensive anxieties and concentrate on giving the Axis army a damaging reverse on ground where they had been preparing their defenses for some time past.

Rommel quickly forced his way round Bir Hacheim and northeast behind the Eighth Army defenses as the first stage of a drive toward Tobruk. But here Eighth Army's armored counterattack forces were able to hold him, and the shock success of his initial outflanking thrust, having failed to retain its first momentum, created problems for him. He was now confined with his back to the British minefield and wire, without a line of communication, and being counterattacked by the British armor. To extricate himself from a situation that could have been fatal, if the British had properly exploited it, he had to open a line of communication back through the British minefield, while beating off the attacks which Eighth Army, recovering from its initial disruption, was directing against him.

If General Ritchie had been able to gather his superior number of armored formations for a concentrated counterattack he could have won a decisive victory. Unfortunately the besetting weakness of the Eighth Army—dispersion of effort, or "too few too late"—again manifested itself. The armored formations were brought to the counterattack severally. In turn Rommel defeated them until by June 12, after three weeks' hard fighting, he had reduced Eighth Army's tank strength to 70 while his own tanks still numbered 160, including 100 German; this despite the success of the new

Grants with their 75-mm. guns which had taken the Germans by surprise and had wrought considerable damage.

The crucial tank battle having been settled in his favor, Rommel moved on to Tobruk which, after two days' hard fighting, he captured on June 21, with 35,000 prisoners and a considerable quantity of material. The next day Rommel, who was forty-nine, heard that a grateful Fuehrer had made him a field-marshal. His comment was typical: "I would rather he had given me one more division!"[11]

The familiar headlong chase back to the Egyptian frontier now took place—the "Benghazi Handicap" as the desert soldiers had irreverently been calling it in the past two years. General Ritchie decided to make his next stand at Mersa Matruh. Four days after Tobruk, Field-Marshal Rommel, triumphant but tired, and down to his last 44 tanks, made contact with Ritchie's forces as they hurriedly took up new defense stations south of this watering place where Antony had once dallied with Cleopatra.

Now, for the second time in a year, General Auchinleck had to resolve a crisis of leadership in the Eighth Army by dismissing the commander. On the first occasion he had intervened decisively to save the successful CRUSADER offensive from being called off through a failure of resolution at the top. This time Auchinleck decided that the wider responsibility of C-in-C Middle East was insignificant compared with the immediate and urgent task of stopping Rommel and saving Egypt. Once again he accepted the distasteful task of replacing the army commander but this time he assumed command himself. It took him only a short time to realize that there was no hope of making a stand at Mersa Matruh and he quickly directed that El Alamein, a station on the coastal road another 100 miles back, was where the soldiers of the Eighth Army— the beaten and exhausted ones streaming back from the Gazala battle; the fresh and rested ones from the Nile Delta—would stand and stop the Panzerarmee Afrika. Having stopped the enemy, Gen. Auchinleck would then turn and attack him, for the Panzerarmee Afrika was not much less exhausted than the Eighth, and after the long advance it was almost out of gasoline. The relentless law of desert warfare was now operating against Rommel. The more victorious he was, the more difficult it became to sustain his lengthening supply line. The point has been made that long desert pursuits were almost as exhausting to the victor as to the vanquished, with the additional difficulty for the victor of extended communications. The Panzerarmee Afrika was by now desperately short of gasoline.

By July 1 Rommel had been effectively stopped by a hurriedly occupied and incomplete defensive system that took its name from the adjacent railway station of El Alamein 60 miles from Alexandria. Through July he made desperate efforts to break through these last few miles to complete a victory that would have been calamitous for Britain. Mussolini flew to Libya with his favorite white charger and stood by in readiness for a Roman entry into Alexandria and Cairo. But Auchinleck frustrated all these efforts by a mobile attacking defense within his defensive position at El Alamein, while trying desperately to rally and inspire the Eighth Army to put enough punch into these attacks to exploit the vulnerability of the Panzerarmee Afrika's extended supply line and perhaps still snatch victory from defeat. But the Eighth Army was too tired. By the end of the month the first battle of Alamein had ended with Rommel still 60 tantalizing miles from Alexandria, the great prize. Auchinleck had for the time being saved Egypt and the Middle East. Because of what was at stake, and the nearness of Rommel to complete success, it was really a considerable victory though at the time it seemed more like an extremely narrow escape.

So the desert war had come to El Alamein, the crucible in which its climactic ordeal would have to take its course. Here on the threshold of Egypt Rommel had been stopped. Here in proper time the British Eighth Army would have to destroy him or itself be destroyed.

It was no accident that this was the place where the campaign came to rest after its breathless fluctuations; no chance whim of fortune that this turned out to be the place of decision where the final trial of strength would take place. At first sight this stretch of desert was no different from any other. It was apparently the same expanse of flatness varied only by the same occasional ridges and mounds, one or two corresponding depressions, some outcrops of rock mainly along the ridges, one or two freak heights, and patches of camel scrub.

But this stretch of desert *was* different. From a military point of view it was unique. It was the only area of the desert battleground where there were two secure flanks. As elsewhere there was the sea flank in the north. But also, 38 miles south of the coast, there was the Qattara Depression: a sunken area of quicksands and salt marsh, 200 feet below sea level; impassable to vehicles, and protected on its north side by 600-foot cliffs.

The mobile tactics of desert warfare had evolved from there normally being only one secure flank, the sea. The offensives launched by both sides had hitherto been based on the whirlwind outflanking attack round the open south flank of the adversary which the desert offered everywhere else but here. These were the tactics with which Rommel had brought the war to the threshold of Cairo and Alexandria. This 38-mile stretch of desert between the sea and the Qattara Depression was the only ground where these tactics could not be applied and where a defense line could be prepared.

The British had of course known about this from their prewar experience of garrisoning Egypt. They knew it as the El Alamein position from the adjacent two-shack railway station 60 miles from Alexandria. It was a piece of ground that from routine reconnaissance they had always known to be potentially important to any defense of Egypt from a western invader. It was, so to say, in the files.

They had carried out peacetime maneuvers there. They knew it well. When General Auchinleck became Commander-in-Chief Middle East in 1941, therefore, one of his first actions had been to give orders for the El Alamein line to be strengthened by some engineer-prepared positions as a routine precautionary measure for tightening up the defense of Egypt. When he stopped Rommel there a year later he was only doing so in the area long recognized by the British Army as the one where a last-ditch stand against an invader of Egypt would inevitably take place—if the defense of Egypt came to this extreme contingency.

Therefore, a decisive battle at El Alamein was virtually preordained.

THE THRESHOLD OF EGYPT

2 THESE FIRST two years of the desert war in which the
battle had commuted, at times almost hysterically, between the
rival goal lines in Egypt and Cyrenaica had taught some hard
lessons. The first was that this was a fast-moving new type
of war, for professionals trained to think and act quickly,
trained to work closely together in a complete mobile har-
mony of armor, infantry and artillery. Bravery was not
enough. It was knowledge born of experience and training that
counted.

Although the Eighth Army had enjoyed a numerical superiority of tanks from the CRUSADER offensive of November 1941 onward they had had the worst of the campaign to
date and indeed had come perilously close to defeat.

The young men who fought these early tank battles were
paying for the failure of the British military hierarchy between the two world wars to devise a coherent tank policy or
doctrine, or even a satisfactory tank. This was ironical because
it was Britain who had invented the tank and introduced it to
the battlefield in 1916. Between the wars, however, it was
Germany who recognized the dominating influence the tank

would exert in the Second World War, and had acted and prepared accordingly. There was a double irony in this, for to whom did the German General Staff turn for the grammar of the new armored warfare? To the British military writers Major-General J. F. C. Fuller and Captain B. H. Liddell Hart, whose theories exerted a greater influence on military thinking in Germany than they did in Britain.

The Germans experimented with these theories of armored warfare in their training, tried them out in the Spanish Civil War, and brought their practice to maturity in Poland and France in 1940. The debt did not go unacknowledged. Rommel's Chief of Staff Lieut.-General Fritz Bayerlein has written: "Of all military writers, it was Liddell Hart who made the deepest impression on the Field-Marshal—and greatly influenced his tactical and strategic thinking."[1]

By contrast the British had barely started to practise tank warfare by 1939. The composition of the tank arm itself was a characteristic British compromise. It was formed by mechanizing the cavalry and combining it with the battalions of the Royal Tank Corps, which dated from the tanks of the First World War. It was not surprising that hussars, dragoons, lancers and county yeomanry regiments (largely officered by the fox-hunting gentry of the English counties) experienced some initial difficulty in adjusting an inherited cavalry tradition of many generations—not to mention an almost ritualistic devotion to the horse as such—to the change. Small wonder that they clung to the last to their cavalry terminology, speaking of "chargers" and "lead horses" and "stables," and thus resisting as long as possible the process of becoming tank-minded. Small wonder that this oversimplified conception of tanks as horses in armor-plating led, in the early desert days, to a costly tendency to make cavalry charges as in the past. These tank men had to learn the hard way that it was pressing the cavalry analogy too far to tackle the German 88-mm. antitank gun screens while using their ancestors of the Light Brigade as their model.

In these early days, too, the British tanks were inferior in firepower, at least to the best of the German machines, and they were mechanically less reliable. Not until the American Grants and later the Shermans appeared (the Shermans came in time for Second Alamein) could the heaviest German tanks be tackled on equal terms.

The dilatoriness of the British Army in formulating a constructive policy of tank warfare between the world wars was deplorable, but it only reflected the flaccid escapism of a public opinion lulled by the appeasement policy of its leaders and by the emotional blandishments of a facile pacifism.

On the other hand, in noting the more realistic appraisal by the German generals of what was going to be required, it should not be overlooked that in this situation a ruthless totalitarian power, deliberately preparing for vengeful conquest, has a distinct advantage over a peace-loving democracy, fumbling its defense budgets, neglecting its peacetime armed forces, and civilized enough since 1918 to regard war as a catastrophe. Military historians in pursuit of objective wisdom after the event are apt to forget this.

The Second World War was something more than a series of field trials to discover the best method of using a tank as a weapon of war. By any standard that matters, it was not to the discredit of the Royal Armoured Corps that, amateurs though they were and unskilled as they were bound to be, they rode in those difficult early desert days with gaiety and panache to a canned death by roasting or frying—as if in expiation of what their leaders had done or left undone in the years before. To say that they took time to become professional is fairer than to be impatient with their early failures. This, too, was part of what Alamein was about.

It was a colorful army, representative of all the British

nations, that underwent this harsh probation in the desert. Of
their own volition and from all directions the imperial cousins
had converged on Egypt. From Australia, New Zealand, South
Africa and India came divisions out of whose deeds the
eventual legend of the Eighth Army would be woven. From
the United Kingdom came some of Britain's best infantry, the
Guards and the Greenjackets, and the tough north-country-
men; from England also came the armored cavaliers of the
new tank formations, the proud hussars and lancers and dragoons who had exchanged their spurs for spanners. (Since
Italy's entry into the war British ships bringing these troops
had to use the long sea route to Egypt round the Cape of
Good Hope and the Red Sea, adding 45 days to the journey.
This was an important factor in the maintenance of the desert
front from the United Kingdom.)

These various groups, with a common purpose and basic
approach but highly individual in their temperaments and prej-
udices, shared together the empirical years in the desert and
helped to fashion the shape of the war that evolved from it. A
war unlike any other. A war of mercurial maneuver and
dynamic outflanking in which the attack came tearing round
the back of the enemy position from the open inland spaces of
the desert, this inland southern flank that was always blandly
and beguilingly open to the attacker.

With no obstacles and few landscape features of any significance to interfere with free and rapid movement, this fast-
flowing campaign was like naval warfare on a petrified sea.
Movement had to be plotted by dead reckoning. The map grid
more often than not covered a completely blank space on the
desert maps. The commander of a squadron of tanks would be
guided to a target like a flotilla of destroyers. In the early days
at least, he seldom had much idea of the over-all army plan or
even the intention. He would receive no more than a wire-
lessed order to go so many miles on a bearing of X degrees,

take up a defensive position facing this way or that, and engage any enemy tanks observed.

In his book Robert Crisp, a South African tank officer, has given a vivid impression of what the CRUSADER offensive was like for a squadron commander.[2] At this level of the fighting it was by no means the spectacular clash conjured up by accounts of the large forces of tanks engaged. This applies of course to any battle. But the spread of a great armored battle in the desert could be eighty miles wide. It was a kind of gigantic chess game on the move which the army commander had to play by remote control. It was understandable that Rommel, finding this remote control impossible, always positioned himself close to his spearhead and ran the battle from there. This exasperated and often alarmed his staff who for hours on end did not know where he was, but it enabled him to react quickly to the changing situation and give new orders there and then. This flexibility was never achieved by the early Eighth Army commanders with their slow, unshakable orthodoxy and their inability to set any new plan in motion without prior conferences.

So "the desert," like "the trenches" in 1914–18, became a comprehensive definition not only of a specialized kind of warfare but of a distinctive way of life. A summary of a tank crew's day may give some idea of what the life was like.[3]

The tank men were generally awakened at about 0500 hours, some time before daylight, so as to be able to drive out of their night lagers to battle or patrol positions by first light after having washed and breakfasted.

Battles commonly occurred in the early morning or in the late afternoon. This was because the armies faced each other on a north-south line which meant that early and late in the day one side could take advantage of the other's having a blinding sun in its eyes—early morning was advantageous for the British, late afternoon for the Axis army. Fighting seldom took place in the middle of the day as the heat haze was then so great that accurate fire was difficult if not impossible. When actual fighting did take place it did not normally last for more than three hours of daylight. The rest of the time was spent by the crews on watch or patrolling or in preparing to attack or to receive an attack. Like their comrades of the other arms the tank men found the long periods of alert expectancy more nerve-wracking and fatiguing than actual battle. It was particularly tiring for tank commanders in the unrelenting heat of the desert because in order to retain immediate all-round vision they were forced to keep their heads above open turrets. This meant standing, as the tank seats in service in the summer of 1942 could not be adjusted to a height that made it possible to sit and peer out of the turret.

Occasionally it was possible for one or two of the crew to get out and stretch their legs or make tea, but it was not unusual for crews to remain in their tanks for an entire period of daylight. The fumes and noise of guns and engines and the need to wear headphones all day greatly added to the strain, fatigue and general unpleasantness.

It was generally 2100 hours or later (at least in the summer months) before the opposing tanks gradually drew apart and at last went off to find their night lagers. This frequently meant another two or three hours of night driving to reach a point conveniently placed for the next day's battle. Having reached the lager they had first to refuel and load up with ammunition from their supply column, a proceeding which took between one-and-a-half and two hours; then they had to carry out maintenance and small running repairs on their tank and distribute rations. It was not often that they could bed down for the night much before an hour after midnight, and even then they were not completely finished, for each man had to do an hour's guard duty during the night. Three hours' sleep was therefore the most that the men could hope for, and senior tank officers reckoned that a week was as long as crews could be expected to go on fighting with efficiency in these rigorous conditions—yet in the summer fighting of 1942 when Rommel was sweeping all before him, some tank units were in action almost continuously for periods up to three weeks. It was an infantry illusion that tank fighting was comparatively comfortable because the combatants rode everywhere and were protected by armor-plating.

It needs little imagination and empathy to discern the pain and the blood beyond this plain description; the mosaic of endurance and scarcely bearable discomfort made up of a thousand tiny unrecorded epics; the white-hot flame tongues of solid shot unbelievably penetrating thick armor, and the implications of this for those inside; the demented ricochet within the steel trap, the spattered brains, the torn entrails of a gunner impossible to extricate; the charred skulls and calcinated bodies of boys who seconds before were alive and beautiful.

These quintessentially were the desert fighters, burnished red-brown and dust-caked like clowns; as their mud-slimed fathers, sodden and lousy and putrid with trench feet, had been quintessentially the trench fighters of the earlier war.

This is what the desert was like for both sides. Out of the shared ordeal came a shared mystique. Not an Eighth Army mystique for the British and a Panzerarmee Afrika mystique for the Germans and Italians, but a collective one that began to embrace both sides. To be "in the desert" became the important thing, the real bond. Between the soldiers of warring armies who fight a long way from home there sometimes grows a spontaneous affinity, a feeling that in their shared plight they have more in common with one another than they have with their own kind at home who sent them to fight. The rival desert armies were not exactly on terms of affection. But the bond of the desert was certainly now felt by both sides. They even shared the same war song "Lilli Marlene," a German song on which neither the Italians nor the British could improve. Also it was a remarkably chivalrous campaign: possibly the last in history. Both sides fought to the limit but within the then accepted rules of war. There is little evidence that either side spoiled the record. The absence of German SS units was a help. One hesitates to press analogy too far, romantic analogy at that, but the facts do seem to support the suggestion that in the desert the flower of chivalry on either side brought to twentieth-century armor the knightly bearing of their mediaeval forebears. The goodness within the battle is war's greatest paradox, but when it is there it should be recorded.

The British, as is their way, went further and came to regard the desert as a kind of club. Membership was limited to those who fought in the desert. There was a private club language in which bastard soldier-Arabic did what bastard soldier-French had done for the troops of the previous world war. Instead of *napoo* for *il n'yen a plus* ("there's nothing to be done," "that's the lot") the variegated accents of London, Liverpool, Glasgow, Sydney, Christchurch and Durban augmented the hubbub of the Cairo streets with their own version of *"Mahleesh"* the Arabic shoulder-shrugging equivalent of "Couldn't matter less!" or "Take a *shufti*" meaning "have a look." An expression in common usage was the faintly contemptuous "white knees" denoting a new arrival from England. The burnishing to which the desert submitted those who came to it to fight was so deep that white knees could look obscenely white. If their owner happened to be a general who had come out to command a division his task was just that much harder until, his knees having conformed like everyone else's, he could begin to persuade these independent British, many of whom had been no nearer to Britain than this Western Desert, that he was "one of them" and a proper person to be leading them.

In dress the club were casual to a degree that would have

caused apoplectic fits in England's citadels of military recti-
tude. Except when dressed for combat—tropical shorts, shirt,
with the addition of a woollen cardigan at night—the men
generally wore nothing more than shorts and boots.

Officers were scarcely less casual. The flexible suede
"desert boots" entered the vocabulary of English-style foot-
wear in the desert and have remained there ever since. The
other sartorial symbol of the desert was the vividly colored
silk neck scarf—functional in respect of dust and sweat, pretty
for the hell of it. This fashion crossed no man's land, the
colored scarf being adopted also by the German officers including their redoubtable commander Rommel, who wore his
Iron Cross under one.

The desert boots and the colored silk scarf were the em-
blematic musts of desert officer dress. On this foundation the
cavalry regiments, immemorially the supreme exponents of
military high fashion, could devise their own last touches of
chic. The khaki drill-type shirt made to measure in better
material; honey-colored corduroy trousers; sheepskin coats;
Not regulation of course but much more elegant, and so long
as the regiment's officers were all dressed alike, what did it
matter?

All this—trivial though it now seems—contributed to the
potent sense of identity that the Eighth Army was developing.
But perhaps the most curious thing about this club was that its
unofficial honorary vice-president was the enemy Commander-
in-Chief!

Rommel was, among other things, clever at public relations. He gained a reputation for chivalrous informality with
the captured, making a point of talking to any captured British
wounded he found in his own hospitals. His staff, whom he
drove hard, said that he was more considerate to his captured
enemies than he was to them! This plus the spectacular tear-
away manner in which he achieved his successes with the
dynamic spearhead he had fashioned out of the two panzer

divisions of the Afrika Korps and the by now nearly as celebrated 90th Light Division, had won him something akin to a
fan club in Eighth Army and helped to complete the Rommel legend. He was apparently not only an invincible military
genius but also he was that epitome of high British esteem "a
decent chap"!

In the meantime Eighth Army had seen two army commanders of its own dismissed and it had only been saved from
disaster by Auchinleck at the last defensible position before
the Nile.

The Rommel legend was certainly a potent force and
even the levelheaded and pragmatical Auchinleck had recognized its importance and danger some time before. Rommel's
biographer Desmond Young quotes an order Auchinleck had
thought necessary to issue to all commanders and chiefs of
staff:

> There exists a real danger that our friend Rommel is be-
> coming a kind of magician or bogey-man to our troops, who
> are talking far too much about him. He is by no means a
> superman, although he is undoubtedly very energetic and able.
> Even if he were a superman, it would still be highly undesira-
> ble that our men should credit him with supernatural pow-
> ers.
>
> I wish you to dispel by all possible means the idea that
> Rommel represents something more than an ordinary German
> general. The important thing now is to see to it that we do not
> always talk of Rommel when we mean the enemy in Libya.
> We must refer to "the Germans" or "the Axis powers" or
> "the enemy" and not always keep harping on Rommel.
>
> Please ensure that this order is put into immediate effect,
> and impress upon all Commanders that, from a psychological
> point of view, it is a matter of the highest importance.
>
> (*signed*)   C. J. Auchinleck
> General,
> Commander-in-Chief, Middle East Forces.[4]

It must have been the first time in a major war that the commanding general of a national army found it necessary to issue an order to the effect that admiration of the opposing commanding general would cease forthwith! But despite the order the Rommel fan club persisted incorrigibly.

That had been some time before. In the July fighting at El Alamein—First Alamein as the historians have named it—Auchinleck had tackled not the legend but the reality. By the end of July the reality had conceded victory in these words:

> Although the British losses in this Alamein fighting had been higher than ours, yet the price to Auchinleck had not been excessive, for the one thing that mattered to him was to halt our advance, and that, unfortunately, he had done.[5]

The British losses had in fact totaled 13,000 killed, wounded and missing. Rommel had certainly been stopped—but had the legend?

The Rommel legend was still riding high—to the plaintive strains of "Lilli Marlene"—when Winston Churchill decided to visit Egypt and to make drastic changes in this favored Eighth Army on which so much had been lavished but which had failed so sadly to come up to expectations.

In August, accompanied by Chief of the General Staff General Sir Alan Brooke (later Field-Marshal Lord Alanbrooke), he flew to Egypt and made the clean sweep of the Middle East command that he had been contemplating since the disasters of the early summer. General Sir Harold (later Field-Marshal Earl) Alexander was to be the new Commander-in-Chief Middle East Forces, and General (later Field-Marshal Viscount) B. L. Montgomery would command the British Eighth Army.

At first the Eighth Army command had been given to Lieutenant-General W. H. E. Gott—against the advice of Brooke who favoured Montgomery. Gott was the most senior of the original desert veterans and popular with the army, but

Brooke's impression was that he was too tired and stale to take on the job. An impression confirmed by Gott himself who told Brooke, "I think what is required out here is some new blood. I've tried most of my ideas. . . . We need someone with new ideas and plenty of confidence in them."[6] Fate now intervened. On the day after his appointment an unescorted air transport in which Gott was traveling to take up his new appointment was shot down. Montgomery, then in England, was ordered to fly to the Middle East immediately.

On August 15 the new team took over.

Auchinleck was unlucky in having to step down after his magnificent effort of rallying the Eighth Army and stopping Rommel within a few miles of his great prize. He was unlucky in the failure of his subordinates to measure up to the exacting standards imposed by a virtuoso enemy, but when this has been said it must also be made clear that it was by his own choice that his talent and energy had for so long been wasted on the higher and more proconsular responsibility of theater commander instead of in commanding the field army—the more important job in these years, and the one for which his recent performance had shown him best suited. As far back as December 1941, Churchill had urged him to consider taking personal command of the Eighth Army and he had declined.[7]

In June after the fall of Tobruk Auchinleck himself had envisaged his replacement in a letter to the Chief of the Imperial General Staff:

The unfavourable course of the recent battle in Cyrenaica culminating in the disastrous fall of Tobruk impels me to ask you seriously to consider the advisability of retaining me in my command. . . . Personally I feel fit to carry on and reasonably confident of being able to turn the tables on the enemy in time. All the same there is no doubt that in a situation like the present, fresh blood and new ideas at the top may make all the difference.[8]

If this letter to General Brooke is considered alongside the thoughts lately confided to Brooke by Gott, can there be any doubt that the decision to give the Middle East Command and its army a new deal was the right one? The only questionable part of it was the Prime Minister's insistence, against advice, on choosing the tired Gott—a mistake fortunately, if somewhat drastically, rectified by Providence.

UNDER NEW MANAGEMENT

3   THE TWO NEW COMMANDERS, whose partnership was to make history, provided a sharp contrast in personality. Harold Alexander was a charming, good-looking patrician with all the easy assurance of his upper-class background—Harrow, Cambridge, the Guards—but with this went the talent and the quality that enables a man to rise to the top of his profession without appearing to try. He was born, it might be said, with a silver field-marshal's baton in his knapsack. He had the air of a *grand seigneur*—but also the manner of an infinite professional. His initiation in war had been as a junior officer in the Flanders mud of 1914–18. His baptism in senior command had been provided by the unhappy operations that had culminated in Dunkirk and the recent retreat before the Japanese in Burma. Alexander had emerged from these trials with an enviable reputation for imperturbability when things were going badly, and for apparent fearlessness under fire.

Bernard L. Montgomery was a different proposition. Wiry, sharp-featured and with a high dry voice, he had none of the more obvious characteristics of the soldier-hero. He was a dedicated commander who believed that war was the con-

summation of the soldier's purpose; who affirmed, significantly, that of the great captains of history the two he most
admired were Moses and Cromwell. Unlike the favored Alexander he was of the unmoneyed Victorian middle class, a par-
son's son, the fourth of a family of nine children born to the
wife of a London clergyman of Northern Irish antecedents.
He had had a rigorous Victorian upbringing in a household
dominated by a severe mother whose discipline seems to have
been based equally on the Bible and the cane. Montgomery has
described his childhood as lonely and loveless and has suggested that this was the basic spur to his ambition.[1]

From the first he had approached the profession of soldiering with the dedicated detachment of a monk, excluding
women from his life on the grounds that they did not go with
a serious career as a soldier. (Not until he was thirty-eight did
he marry. Then he addressed himself to marriage with ruthless
application until, after ten happy years, his wife died; a blow
which left him more determinedly single-minded about his job
than ever.) As a young officer posted to regimental duty in
India he had noted with disapproval that most officers at that
time (1908) "went to India to drink gin, play polo and have a
good time."[2] He had been scornful of this majority, who had
private means and regarded soldiering as no more than a congenial and easy occupation, being himself one of the minority
who had to live on his pay. Accordingly from the first he
involved himself as little as possible in army social activity and
lived only for his work. In a sphere where academic indolence
was common, he courted unpopularity by his seriousness of
purpose. In his personal habits he was austere to the point of
asceticism: a teetotaler and nonsmoker who read the Bible
every day and went to bed early.

In Britain in 1941 he had acquired a fearsome reputation
as a corps commander for the realism (to the point of casualties) of his training, his ruthless sacking of commanding offi-

cers who failed to come up to his exacting standards, and for
his fanaticism about physical fitness. He had laid down that in
his corps all officers under forty would carry out a cross-
country run every week, his own staff included. If they were
to drop dead from the exertion, he told them, it was better
that they should do so as soon as possible and not wait until
they were in battle.

He had no illusions about himself. "One has to be a bit
of a cad to succeed in the Army," he has said. "I am a bit of
a cad."[3]

"Monty?" Churchill once said to Alexander, with a
chuckle, "Monty's on the make."[4]

They could hardly have been more different from one
another: Alexander the affable cavalier, Montgomery the uncompromising roundhead. Yet they made an ideal team, as
their virtues and defects were complementary, and there was
never any question of jealousy clouding their working relationship. It was Montgomery's job to win the battles: Alexander's to be the impresario and provide him with everything
he needed from tanks and men to moral support in his dealings
with an impatient Prime Minister. This was understood by
both men from the start. There was never any difficulty between them over who got the credit for what.

Alexander's orders to Montgomery were simple: Destroy
the Axis forces in Africa.

The new army commander soon made his presence felt.
He moved Eighth Army Headquarters to a site by the sea
alongside Desert Air Force Headquarters so that there should
be the closest co-operation between air and ground forces—
the principle of side-by-side command which later became
axiomatic. Until then it had by no means been the rule, and
certainly had not been observed by Montgomery's predecessors.

He put in hand the assembling (from spare formations not

at present in the line) of a new *corps de chasse* of two armored divisions to be kept as a striking reserve and which he hoped eventually to use as Rommel used his Afrika Korps.

He issued uncompromising orders that there would be no more withdrawal; the battle for Egypt would be fought—to the death if necessary—in the Alamein line.

He visited front-line units and talked to as many officers and men as possible. The visits and the sharp questions were purposeful and businesslike and the new general made a particularly good impression on the tough and skeptical Australians and New Zealanders whose commanders—being responsible first to their own governments—enjoyed somewhat more independence than their United Kingdom colleagues, and consequently had to be handled on occasion more delicately.

Montgomery's flair for showmanship, which later became a feature of his behavior, was at this time in its infancy: though he did have one publicity success—which incidentally, gave a foretaste of things to come—when he accepted from the Australians one of their wide-brimmed bush hats: a gesture which not only did much to captivate the Australian troops but was worth a large number of press photographs. This publicity performed the valuable service of making Montgomery's face familiar to the entire Eighth Army in the shortest possible time. Eighth Army was now commanded by a general who was something of a character—and before long every man knew it.

About Montgomery's first days with the Eighth Army a somewhat exaggerated legend came into being at the time—a magic transformation of a beaten and dispirited force into a New Model army of shining-eyed crusaders. The legend of course exaggerated. But also exaggerated was the counter-legend subsequently developed by some commentators who sought to diminish Montgomery's achievement by suggesting that he was a showman who merely executed plans inherited from his predecessors; a lucky general who came on the scene when for the first time there was plenty of everything that an army could need—unlike the earlier commanders who had had to fight the campaign (it is suggested) on a shoestring. The counter-legend is as exaggerated as the legend, for the record, as we have seen, shows quite clearly that from Auchinleck's first offensive of 1941 Eighth Army always enjoyed a substantial superiority of tanks and guns.

If it be argued that legend and counter-legend have no place in military history the answer must be that they do sometimes and Alamein is one of the times. For this is a battle whose full implications cannot be understood unless some account is given of the emotional and personal background.

It will not be out of place, therefore, to reaffirm there is an abundance of reliable evidence that the immediate impact of Montgomery on the Eighth Army was beneficial to an exceptional degree. Two witnesses of particular significance may be quoted.

Brigadier (later Maj.-Gen. Sir Howard) Kippenberger—who subsequently commanded the New Zealand Division—was fifty-five (the same age as Montgomery), a veteran of World War One, and in civilian life a lawyer. After the war he became the editor-in-chief of the *New Zealand Official War History*, a position he held with distinction until his death in 1958. From every point of view he can be considered a balanced observer. This is his account of Montgomery's first visit to the New Zealanders in the Alamein line:

I saw him first when he called, unannounced, a few days after his arrival. He talked sharply and curtly, without any soft words, asked some searching questions . . . and left me feeling very much stimulated. For a long time we had heard little from Army except querulous grumbles that the men should not go about without their shirts on . . . or things of that sort. Now we were told that we were going to fight, there

was no question of retirement to any reserve positions or anywhere else. . . . To make the intention clear our troop-carrying
transport was sent a long way back so that we could not run
away if we wanted to! There was no more talk of the alternative positions in the rear. We were delighted, and the morale
of the whole Army went up incredibly.[5]

The enemy were equally impressed. Major-General F. W.
von Mellenthin, one of Rommel's chief staff officers, wrote:

There can be no question that the fighting efficiency of
the British improved vastly under the new leadership, and for
the first time Eighth Army had a commander who really made
his will felt throughout the whole force. . . . Auchinleck was
an excellent strategist with many of the qualities of a great
commander, but he seems to have failed in tactical detail, or
perhaps in ability to make his subordinates do what he wanted
. . . his offensives later in the month (i.e. in July during the
first battle of Alamein) were costly, unsuccessful, and from
the tactical point of view extremely muddled.

General von Mellenthin goes on to say:

Montgomery is undoubtedly a great tactician—circumspect
and thorough in making his plans, utterly ruthless in carrying
them out. He brought a new spirit to Eighth Army, and illus-
trated once again the vital importance of personal leadership in
war.[6]

So the Eighth Army and its new commander prepared for
their first task: to resist the new attempt which they knew
Rommel must make to break through to the Nile. They were
pretty certain they knew when it would be made—on or
shortly after August 25, when the moon would be full. They
had a pretty good idea where the attack would come.

Montgomery had accepted in principle the defense plan
devised by his predecessor.[7] Its basis was a strong defense of
the Alamein line from the coast to south of the Ruweisat

Ridge by four infantry divisions, the ten-mile gap from the left of these positions to the Quattara Depression being covered by a minefield, behind which lay the 7th (Light) Armoured Division in a mobile defensive role.

He also agreed with the appreciation of the Auchinleck staff that the vital ground in the forthcoming battle would be the Alam el Halfa ridge, five miles long and about five miles behind the main Alamein positions. It was obviously a piece of ground Rommel would have to secure on his way to the coast should he break through the British positions. Like his predecessor Montgomery saw—to any military eye it was obvious—that this was a key feature to hold in strength.

Having accepted from the previous command this outline Montgomery lost no time in impressing his own signature on it. He increased the garrison of Alam el Halfa from one to two brigades. (Alexander was helpful in making this possible.) He stiffened the front-line defenses and summoned more tanks and artillery from the Delta. He initiated some deception measures with dummy tanks and dummy minefields designed to confuse any breakthrough between the New Zealand left and Himeimat, the weaker part of the line where the German attack was expected (and where in fact it did come).

But his particular and crucial addition to the defense plan was his idea to assign the main defense of Alam el Halfa to the 22nd Armoured Brigade—in dug-in hull-down positions just west of the ridge. To quote Field-Marshal Alexander:

"The essence of Montgomery's plan was the digging in, hull down, of the 22nd Armoured Brigade at the foot of Alam el Halfa ridge—while keeping his extreme south flank mobile."[8]

This mobile south flank was in fact the 7th (Light) Armoured Division with strict orders not to get embroiled in a battle when attacked but to harass the attackers and to fall back and lure the German tanks on to the ambush—the killer guns of the dug-in Grants of 22nd Armoured Brigade. In no circumstances was the British armor to be tempted into fighting the Germans in the open.

From the record and from what he had now seen for himself of their standard of training, this (Montgomery considered) was why they had been beaten by Rommel so often before. This was to be a static defensive battle and this was entirely Montgomery's notion, not that of his predecessor who had laid down that the Alamein defenses would be "fluid and mobile" which meant that the tanks would have risked just that encounter in the open with the more skillful panzers that Montgomery was determined to avoid until his own tanks were better trained.

For Rommel August had been a frustrating month aggravated by illness (chronic stomach and intestinal catarrh, nasal diphtheria and high blood pressure) and failure to persuade the Commando Supremo in Rome or his own High Command to improve his supply position. Some idea of what he was up against may be gained from the fact that in July he had received only a fifth of what he needed.

His constant complaints to Rome seem to have had some justification. There were 42,000 Germans in the desert compared with 82,000 Italians, yet in the first three weeks of August the German element of the Panzerarmee received only 8,200 tons of supplies (32 per cent of what they asked for) while the Italians received 25,700. Admittedly the Italian allotment included 800 tons for civilian needs and the *Luftwaffe* also received 8,500 tons. Even so the disproportionate allocations clearly favored the Italians. And with his own front-line 164th Division down to 60 vehicles it cannot have sweetened Rommel's temper to see a new Italian division, the Pistoia, arrive in Libya with nearly 400 vehicles although it was not even intended for service at the front.

The Axis were paying the penalty now for their failure to subdue Malta, for this thorn in their side was the base from which the Royal Navy and Royal Air Force were crippling their efforts to convoy Rommel's supplies from Sicily to Benghazi and Tripoli. Hitler had shrunk from the Malta operation that had been planned; and Rommel, against the advice of his staff, and the Italian Commando Supremo had agreed with Hitler's decision, preferring to stake everything on the headlong dash for Egypt in the summer. It was a notable case of the gambler in Rommel, so attractive to his more romantic admirers, fatally swaying his military judgment.[9]

Having been thwarted a few miles from his goal Rommel was now saddled with an extended supply line that made it almost impossible to prepare adequately for a new attack. Benghazi was 650 miles away, Tripoli 1,400. A great quantity of the precious gasoline, his greatest need, that did manage to run the gauntlet of the Sicilian narrows had then to be used up by the supply trucks bringing it forward to where it was wanted—and these vulnerable columns of transport were subject to continuous attack by an air force daily growing stronger.[10] This was not a happy situation in which to be trying to mount an offensive. Illness and the extreme heat of the Egyptian summer cannot have made the days of decision any easier.

The Eighth Army felt certain that they knew when Rommel would make his last bid for Egypt and where. He would have to attack at or shortly after the August full moon which was on the 25th. He would know that he could not risk waiting until a month later with Eighth Army strength piling up all the time. He *must* catch the August moon or give up altogether the idea of completing the conquest of Egypt, and no one thought he would do that.

As for the place where he would launch his offensive, this was bound to be on the southern sector of the line to the south of the New Zealanders. This was the only part of the front where he could possibly hope for a quick penetration and in view of his known shortage of gasoline a quick penetration of the British defenses was essential if he was to give his tank columns a chance to race through to Cairo and Alexandria while they still had enough fuel to get there.

Hence the importance of the Alam el Halfa ridge, the long-stop position on the flank of any breakthrough, where the main battle was bound to take place after the first penetration. Montgomery's revision of its defenses and his plan to lure the panzers into a tank ambush gave everyone in Eighth Army the feeling that this defensive battle was one they would win—for its course was entirely predictable and they would be fighting on ground of their choice to the plan of a new commander who clearly knew most precisely what he was doing.

The application of sporting analogies to war is often a glib oversimplification of what it is really about. It may not in this instance be out of place, however, to suggest that there was a certain portentous drama in the prospect of the new challenger, the astringent roundhead Montgomery, now sitting back to await the onslaught of the reigning champion, the mercurial buccaneer Rommel, at this time the more renowned of the two, but somewhat handicapped by illness.

THE CURTAIN RAISER

4   ROMMEL LAUNCHED the attack, as he was expected to do, on the southern sector of the El Alamein front on the night of August 30. In the matter of time he had cut it a little fine, for the moon was now five days past full, but he had been holding on until the last possible moment, hoping that the additional gasoline stock which Marshal Ugo Cavallero had promised to get across to Benghazi without fail would actually arrive. In point of fact the gasoline never did arrive and in the end he had to rely on what he had and the 500 tons that Kesselring had promised to fly to him daily in the event of Cavallero's letting him down. His eve-of-battle anxieties were reflected in this letter he wrote to his wife a few hours before the battle opened:

30 August 1942

Dearest Lu,

    Today has dawned at last. It's been such a long wait worrying all the time whether I should get everything I needed together to enable me to take the brakes off again. Many of my worries have been by no means satisfactorily settled and we have some very grave shortages. But I've taken

the risk, for it will be a long time before we get such favoura-
ble conditions of moonlight, relative strengths, etc., again. . . .
If our blow succeeds it might go some way towards deciding
the whole course of the war. . . .[1]

For this last effort to span the mere 60 miles that lay
between the Panzerarmee Afrika and the supreme prize,
Rommel grouped together the pick of his motorized and
armored forces: the trusty 15th and 21st Panzer Divisions (the
Afrika Korps), 90th Light Division (who had worked with
them so closely and so often in the past as to be virtually a part
of the Afrika Korps), and the Ariete and Littorio armored
divisions of the Italian XX Corps, the best of the Italian
armor.

Rommel would start the battle with 443 tanks—of which
200 were German, including 27 of the formidable new Mark
IV's meeting the Eighth Army for the first time, while 70 of
the Mark III's had been re-equipped with a better gun.[2] The
Italian medium and light tanks were obsolete and would not
amount to a great deal, so that it was the 200 German tanks on
which Rommel would mainly have to rely.

The Eighth Army formations standing by for the engagement had 713 tanks of all types including 164 of the American
Grants, and there were nearly 200 more at hand in the forward
area and more still in the Delta base it required.[3]

Rommel's plan was essentially the one that had succeeded
so many times before, an encirclement from the south round
the British left—but with the vital difference that the southern
flank was this time not the limitless open desert that had served
him so well in the past but the impassable obstacle of the
Qattara Depression. This time he would have to break through
the crust of the British defenses first, he could not go round
them. But within this limitation it was the plan that had succeeded at Gazala in the spring—a swift encirclement by his

armored spearhead to cut off the main front-line British force and roll up the rear before they knew what was happening.

"We placed particular reliance in this plan," Rommel commented significantly, "on the slow reaction of the British command and troops, for experience had shown us that it always took them some time to reach decisions and put them into effect. We hoped, therefore, to be in a position to present the operation to the British as an accomplished fact."[4]

The success of the plan would depend entirely on the speed with which the first penetration of the British line could be made and the encircling force despatched on its way. Rommel was informed by his Intelligence staff that the sector to be attacked—the 8 miles between the New Zealand left at Munassib and the depressions west of Himeimat—was only held by "weakly mined defences."[5] This estimate was to prove fatally wide of the mark.

There were to be three thrusts along the 8-mile front. On the right of the line the two divisions of the Afrika Korps would make the main effort. The two armored divisions of the Italian XX Corps would attack on their left. Further left the 90th Light Division would attack the left of the New Zealand positions.

Influenced mainly by his overly optimistic Intelligence reports but also by his boundless confidence in himself and his Afrika Korps, even to the point of recklessness, Rommel imposed a ruthless timetable. All three attacking groups were to be through the British minefield well before dawn, by which time the Afrika Korps and part of the Italian corps were to be 30 miles beyond it, with the rest of the force lined up on its left. The Afrika Korps would then race for the coast and thus cut the Eighth Army off from its bases, while the infantry dealt with the encircled British front-line formations at leisure. Then the Afrika Korps would split up for the kill—21st Pan-

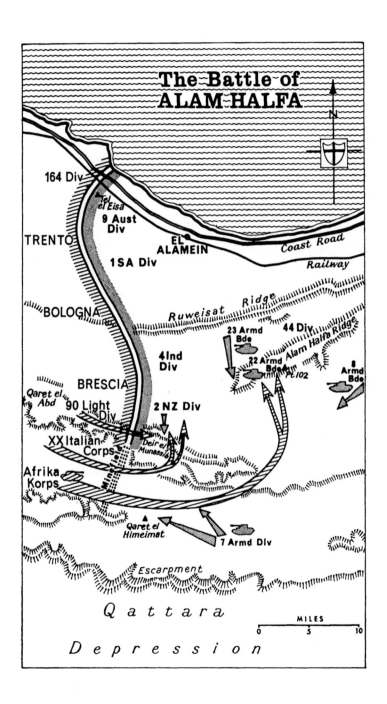

The Battle of ALAM HALFA

N

164 Div

Tel el Eisa

9 Aust Div

TRENTO

EL ALAMEIN

1 SA Div

Coast Road

Railway

BOLOGNA

Ruweisat Ridge

44 Div

23 Armd Bde

22 Armd Bde

Alam Halfa Ridge

8 Armd Bde

Pt 102

4 Ind Div

BRESCIA

Qaret el Abd

90 Light Div

2 NZ Div

Deir el Munassib

XX Italian Corps

Afrika Korps

Qaret el Himeimat

7 Armd Div

Escarpment

Qattara

MILES

0   5   10

Depression

zer Division making for Alexandria, 15th Panzer Division with 90th Light Division heading for Cairo.

What actually happened on the night of August 30 was that the assaulting troops found the British minefield much wider and more intense than Intelligence reports had led them to expect and the British covering parties (provided by the motorized infantry of 7th Armoured Division) much stronger. In the moonlight the artillery of the British division was able to fire to good effect and from the flank the neighboring guns of the 2nd New Zealand Division's artillery also were able to add to the discomfort of the German mine-lifting parties.

The end result was that at dawn, by which time the Afrika Korps was supposed to be 30 miles beyond the British minefield and ready to wheel northward, the German assault troops were still struggling through the minefield. It was 9:30 A.M. before they had the greater part of their armor through to the open and were ready to proceed with the preliminary eastward drive—the commander of the 21st Panzer Division, Major-General G. von Bismarck being killed by mortar fire on the way.

With the arrival of daylight two other things happened. Montgomery was able to piece together from reports of the night's business a picture of the German attack and its probable development, and he alerted and concentrated his armored forces about Alam el Halfa ridge to meet the attack. Secondly, the Desert Air Force took to the air, and relays of medium bombers flying in tight formations of twelve or eighteen carpet-bombed the attacking forces, taking particularly heavy toll of vehicles. A victim of one of these bombing attacks was Major-General W. Nehring, commander of the Afrika Korps, who was wounded.

Meanwhile Rommel, having lost the shock effect of speed and surprise, realized that the offensive had probably failed in the British minefield the night before and considered calling it off there and then. But before doing so, he decided to go forward to the Afrika Korps and confer with Colonel Bayerlein, its chief of staff who had taken command in place of the wounded Nehring. Bayerlein was willing, so Rommel decided that the attack should go on but with a less ambitious thrust line. Instead of the intended wide sweep to the coast 40 miles behind the Alamein line, the Afrika Korps was to make a closer wheel and attack the Alam el Halfa ridge. The reasoning behind this earlier turn to the north was that Montgomery would now have had time to concentrate the bulk of his armored strength about the ridge and with 7th Armoured Division to the south of it the original wide sweep east and north could no longer be undertaken with such armored strength threatening its flank. (Rommel was reacting in fact just as Montgomery had intended.)

Hampered by the repeated bombing attacks and the harassing tactics of the delaying screen of 7th Armoured Division, Colonel Bayerlein was not ready to execute the closer wheel until afternoon, when 21st Panzer Division advanced on Pt. 102 (a feature just off the western end of Alam el Halfa) where the 22nd Armoured Brigade was waiting for them in prepared battle positions just south of the ridge.

It will be remembered that the essence of Montgomery's plan was to use his tanks hull-down in a strictly defensive capacity, and the mainstay of this plan was to be the Grants with their 75-mm. gun. In the flat desert terrain, however, the Grants were not easy to dispose of in this way. Their guns were admittedly superior to any other tank armament in the Eighth Army at this time, but instead of being mounted in the turret they were in a sponson rather low on the front side of the tank. For the gun to have any field of fire, more of the tank's ungainly superstructure than was comfortable had to show itself. For this defensive operation commanders had made the best of it by siting the battle positions of the Grants in broken foothills wherever possible and by bulldozing emplacements for them elsewhere.

A code word had alerted them as soon as the German attack had opened the night before, and long before dawn they were in their battle stations just south of the ridge. At the same time the 8th Armoured Brigade had been ordered to battle positions 10 miles to the southeast of the ridge from which it could attack the flank of any wide sweep that the enemy might attempt (the sweep which Rommel had in fact intended, but had now abandoned).

A second armored brigade, the 23rd, was on the right and to the rear of the 22nd, watching the gap to the west of the ridge.

From dawn the 22nd Armoured Brigade had been waiting tensely for what the day might bring. The tanks were mostly turret-down in their emplacements with their commanders standing on them. When the time came to shoot they would edge forward. Meanwhile they waited, hoping the wait would not be too long and taking heart from the tight formations of bombers passing over with smooth regularity to pound the Panzerarmee Afrika wherever its assault forces and supply columns could be found.

The 22nd knew nothing of the drama on the Axis side that morning: of the wrecking of the panzers' schedule in the British minefields; of the German loss of two senior generals; of the hurried change of plan; of Rommel's agonizing worry about whether his fuel would arrive in time. All they knew was that the Afrika Korps was "out there" not very far away in the fog of dust that tanks, trucks and bombers had created, and to which the desert had for good measure added one of its characteristic sandstorms which from midmorning gave the German-Italian forces some protection from the British bombers and some cover in which to make their advance. The storm added to the discomfort and suspense of the British waiting on or near the ridge for the blow that they knew must come before nightfall. It was late afternoon, about five o'clock, when, eyes straining to pierce the dust-fog, they first sighted the great column of tanks of the 15th and 21st Panzer Divisions which the acting Afrika Korps commander, Bayerlein, had sent to make the first assault on Alam el Halfa. The sound of the sandstorm muffled the roar and clatter with which tanks generally herald their approach and this perhaps made them even more sinister, as they jolted and lurched through the desert.

Modern war seldom accords with the image of it that film producers have so assiduously cultivated through the years. It is diffuse and chaotic and much less conveniently dramatic. But the crucial tank engagement that was now to take place between the Afrika Korps and the British 22nd Armoured Brigade on the second day of Alam el Halfa did come closer than usual to the Hollywood idea of what a battle is like. A vivid picture of it is to be gained from the vantage point of 22nd Armoured Brigade headquarters and the report of its commander, Brigadier (later Major-General) G. P. B. Roberts.

During the day as the reports came in, Brigadier Roberts had been plotting on his map the eastward movement of the enemy. In the early afternoon he ordered two light squadrons to patrol up to 5 miles south of the ridge so as to give him the earliest possible warning of any enemy movement on his front. It was 1530 when the expected signal came back from one of the look-out squadrons: "Strong force of enemy tanks moving northeast."

Roberts continues:

Now I can see the enemy myself through my glasses. They are coming straight up the line of the telegraph posts which lead in front of our position. There is some firing by their leading tanks, presumably at our light squadrons, so I instruct these squadrons to come back—but to take it wide so as not to give our position away.

On they come, a most impressive array. . . . It is fascinating to watch them, as one might watch a snake curl up ready to strike. But there is something unusual too; some of the leading tanks are Mark IV's, and Mark IV's have in the past always had short-barrelled 75-mm. . . . But these Mark IV's have a very long gun on them; in fact it looks the devil of a gun. This must be the long-barrelled stepped-up 75-mm. the Intelligence people have been talking about.[6]

The brigade position was held by three regiments—the 1st Royal Tanks on the right, 4th County of London Yeomanry in the center, and 5th Royal Tanks on the left. Roberts's fourth regiment, the Royal Scots Greys, was about two miles back in reserve behind the ridge. These defenses were reinforced by a number of antitank guns manned by infantrymen, and massive artillery support was available to bring down curtains of defensive fire in front of the brigade positions as and when required.

The Roberts narrative continues:

And now they all turn left and face us and begin to advance slowly. The greatest concentration seems to be opposite the County of London Yeomanry and the antitank guns of the Rifle Brigade. (Eighty-seven German tanks were counted at this time opposite this part of the front.) I warn all units over the air not to fire until the enemy are within 1,000 yards; and then in a few seconds the tanks of the County of London Yeomanry open fire and the battle is on. Once one is in the middle of a battle time is difficult to judge, but it seems only a few minutes before nearly all the tanks of the Grant squadron of the County of London Yeomanry are on fire. The new German 75-mm. is taking a heavy toll. The enemy tanks have halted and they have had their own casualties, but the situation is serious; there is a complete hole in our defence."

Roberts hurriedly signaled his reserve regiment, the Royal Scots Greys, to come forward as quickly as possible to fill the gap that had been blasted in the center of his front by the massacre of the Yeomanry. Meanwhile the German tanks began to edge forward again until they approach a sector held by Rifle Brigade antitank guns. Courageously holding their fire until the panzers are within a few hundred yards the infantrymen knock out several, but some of the guns are overrun by sheer weight of numbers.

It is at this time that the operation takes on the nature of a film Western. Will the "sheriff's posse," the Royal Scots Greys, arrive in time to fill the gap in the front left by the Yeomanry? The panzers are now very close.

Brigadier Roberts invokes the artillery SOS, a defending commander's trump, and almost immediately the fire of every gun within range comes crashing down on the German tanks at the very threshold of the British defenses. This stops them.

But what Roberts wants to know is where are the Greys?

"Come on the Greys," he yells over the radio, "Get out your whips." But there is still no sign of them, the suspense is scarcely bearable, for there is still another half hour of daylight. Roberts is determined not to move either the left-hand or right-hand regiment from its secure position to fill the gap in the center because this will weaken his flanks. In desperation he again calls on the artillery, and again the artillery responds with shattering concentrations just in front of his positions. The panzers are again checked. A little more time has been bought.

And then the Greys come thundering over the crest of the ridge from the north, in a great cloud of dust. "They have not really been long," writes Roberts, "but it has seemed an age. I describe the situation to them over the air as they come in sight of the battlefield and charge down the hill; they are quite clear as to the hole they have to plug and they go straight in. The light is beginning to fade and the situation in the center seems to be stabilized."

At 1730, after a further attempt to infiltrate the British left the enemy withdrew for the night, having lost 22 tanks to the 21 of the British. So ended the Afrika Korps' first effort to capture the Alam el Halfa Ridge. The attack had lasted two hours. Brigadier Roberts's account of its over-all shape from the brigade viewpoint can be supplemented by extracts from reports made by the regiments involved in the fighting.

This was how it seemed to Major Cameron of the County of London Yeomanry, whose squadron took the first fury of the new Mark IV panzers and lost 12 tanks in a few minutes:

. . . well before the German tanks reached the telegraph poles, which we knew to be our maximum effective range, the Germans opened fire and already three tanks of my leading troop on the sugar-loaf were blazing before they had hardly fired a shot. In any event the damage our guns could do at that range would have been negligible; but the Germans came on up to and even past the telegraph poles, by which time, of course, they were under intense fire from all along the line: I saw tank after tank going up in flames or being put out of action, and this including my own when the big gun became unserviceable. However, the German advance was momentarily checked. . . .[7]

The 1st Royal Tanks, on the right of the 22nd Brigade position, came through unscathed after a nerve-wracking afternoon which began at 1700 hours when they sighted the German tank column moving northeastward across their front at a range of 2,000 yards. By 1800 hours the column had halted 1,500 yards away, and 1st Royal Tanks saw the panzers shooting up the County of London Yeomanry on their left. At 1810 they were ordered to open fire on the fifty-odd tanks on their own front and they were in action for the next hour and twenty minutes. This is how Captain B. C. Forster concludes his account of what happened:

> At 1930 hours the enemy broke off the engagement leaving thirteen tanks behind, opposite the regimental position. Our casualties had been nil as the enemy's fire had been mostly Armour Piercing with very little High Explosive landing on the position.
> It has been a long, nerve-wracking day. One felt that at any time the Regiment's position could have been overrun by sheer weight of numbers. . . . This was most probably not so, though. Each tank was in a well-reconnoitred position and had every opportunity of bringing accurate fire to bear. . . . As it turned out no massed assault had to be dealt with and we were enabled to have tanks all along the line moving up at odd intervals to fire a few rounds and then reverse back whilst another tank left or took up the fight.[8]

The tank battle in the late afternoon of August 31 was the climax. By failing to win, Rommel had lost forever his chance of victory in Egypt. Had he been more of a strategist and less of a tactical opportunist (probably his fatal shortcoming as a general) he would have cut his losses and, with an eye to future events and the ever-growing strength of his British opponents, might have immediately put in hand a defense zone some way back that would have given depth to the Alamein position. Instead he insisted on trying again.

Early the next morning, September 1, he ordered the Afrika Korps to make another effort to capture the ridge but using 15th Panzer Division only, as the gasoline shortage was now acute. This attack and a second later in the day proved as abortive as those of the previous day. By now Montgomery, certain that Rommel's objective was in fact the ridge and not the wider sweep which his own earlier dispositions had been designed to counter, ordered the 23rd and 8th Armoured Brigades to close in on the 22nd Armoured Brigade so that a phalanx of some 500 tanks now formed a defensive block concentrated to receive any further attacks on the ridge. At the same time he put in hand an infantry counterstroke designed to cut off the German-Italian striking force by driving southward and closing the gap the Germans had made through the British minefield.

So when, on September 3, he received reports that the enemy had shown signs of withdrawing in the south he reaffirmed that his armor was on no account to be tempted down off the ridge and risk an encounter in the open. Rommel's incipient withdrawal might be a feint designed to draw the British tanks out of their prepared positions and so lure them into one of the swiftly organized tank traps that had been a specialty of the Afrika Korps so often before. Then Montgomery ordered the two-brigade 2nd New Zealand Division, with a British brigade under its command, to attack southward that night in the first stage of the operation that was to close the minefield gap behind the enemy attacking force and put it in the bag.

The 2nd New Zealand Division's attack on the night of September 3 was a failure, and strong counterattacks during the next 36 hours made it clear that Rommel had no intention of allowing himself to be put in the bag. He completed an orderly withdrawal of his advanced forces to a line of high ground between Munassib and Himeimat Hill about 5 miles forward of his earlier positions in the southern sector of the Alamein line. As Rommel clearly intended to make a firm stand in this area, Montgomery called the battle off.

This meant leaving the important observation point of Himeimat (a 600-foot height) in enemy hands, but there was method in this.

It was not merely that to retake the height would have involved mounting a major and undoubtedly costly set-piece attack. It also happened that an elaborate deception plan was already being prepared in connection with the greater battle to come. As events had turned out it suited Montgomery very well for Rommel's observers on Himeimat to have a good view during the next few weeks of some of the measures shortly to be put in hand to trick them. They were welcome to Himeimat.

The battle had lasted six days. It had cost Rommel 2,940 officers and men killed, wounded or taken prisoner; 51 tanks and armored cars totally destroyed, many more damaged; and 700 other vehicles. The British losses were 1,640 officers and men killed, wounded or taken prisoner and 67 tanks.[9]

The British victory was attributable to three factors. First, the strategic success of their naval and air forces in strangling Rommel's sea-borne supply line—three tankers were sunk in two days—so that he had to face a crippling gasoline shortage throughout the battle.

Secondly, tactical air superiority over the battlefield. Montgomery's revised system of army-air co-operation enabled the Desert Air Force to give the Eighth Army closer and deadlier support than ever before. From now on the Desert Air Force was virtually an integral part of the Eighth Army. Rommel himself acknowledged "the paralysing effect which air activity on such a scale had on motorised forces."[10] The carpet-bombing from low altitude by close formations of medium bombers was a new technique that caused very high enemy casualties and was to become dolefully familiar to the German army in the months and years to come. The German troops had already nicknamed them "party rallies" by the end of the battle because the squadrons delivered their loads in the close formation normally reserved for ceremonial occasions.

The third factor in Montgomery's victory was his rigid adherence to his plan to make the tanks fight a defensive battle in prepared positions.

It may have been unadventurous but it made sure of his winning, and in the circumstances this was what was wanted. For the point about Alam el Halfa was that in the circumstances merely by not losing it the British would gain a great victory. Whereas merely by not winning it Rommel would have endured a huge and far-reaching defeat.

Apart from its wider implications, Alam el Halfa had a personal significance for the Eighth Army. It was the first opportunity of the Eighth and their new commander to become properly acquainted.

The rapport between an army and its leader is one of the imponderables of war that cannot be measured in the dry factual terms of academic military history. A moral and psychological link based on mutual trust, it has to grow naturally out of the shared experience of battle. It is a kind of love affair and it cannot be laid on to order. It must be remembered that to the rank and file the army commander is a godlike figure so remote from reality that he has no personal identity. If any soldiers did happen to know what he looked like, it would probably be only because of a recollected pandemonium of cleaning and polishing that had once preceded some occasion when he had visited their unit.

The replacement of one army commander by another means very little to the bulk of the soldiery. One general with a red cap band was much the same as another, and Eighth Army had known more than one change during the ups and downs of the desert campaign. It takes time for an army commander to make himself known to his army, and the best way of accelerating the process is to lead them as soon as possible to a not very arduous victory. Alam el Halfa was ideal for the purpose, since probably the least disagreeable of all operations of war is to sit entrenched in ground of your own choice and, with abundant supplies for all your needs and air superiority overhead, receive the enemy attacks and crush them. This was the stimulating experience that Montgomery and the Eighth Army had just enjoyed together.

So the fateful six-day engagement that marked the end of a bold dream for one general and his army was, for the other, the beginning of a long and historic partnership destined for victory.

THE PREPARATIONS

5 WITH THE preliminaries disposed of, the arena was now set for the climactic struggle that would finally settle the issue, and both sides went on the defensive to make their preparations: the Panzerarmee Afrika in a mood of resignation to the loss of the initiative, the Eighth Army revitalized by success and the growing consciousness that it was now in the charge of a general who seemed very much on top of the situation.

For Montgomery the first thing to be settled was the date of his offensive. On the basis that he must allow for at least a week of hard fighting he reckoned that it would be essential to have seven nights of moonlight—which limited the choice to the full-moon period of September or October. He decided that he could not possibly be ready for the earlier date and therefore selected October 23 as his D-day.

There was at first the inevitable growl of impatience from London when Alexander submitted this date. The timing of the offensive at Alamein was linked with two other important strategic issues: the relief of beleaguered Malta by the recapture of the Cyrenaica airfields and, secondly, the projected invasion (under General Eisenhower) of the other end of North Africa by an Anglo-American landing force on November 8. A key hazard in this new enterprise was the unpredictable reaction of the French in North Africa. The French were likely to be much more amenable if the Anglo-American landing was preceded by a decisive British victory at El Alamein. October 23 would be cutting it a little fine.

It required all the sweet reasonableness of General Alexander (backed up in London by General Brooke) to convince the Prime Minister that the earlier date he wanted was out of the question—Montgomery went so far as to threaten to resign if it were insisted upon. It was one of his rules that he would never start an offensive until he was absolutely ready.

Once the date had been fixed, Montgomery set in motion a most rigorous program of training for the six or seven weeks he now had. His outstanding impression of what he had so far seen of the Eighth Army was that it was insufficiently trained, especially the armor. There were reasons for this. In two years of fighting, a stream of replacements for tank crew casualties had been coming out from England only partly trained and there had never been time to complete their training before they went into action. Secondly, there was a hard core of desert veterans at all levels who had got into bad ways during the campaign's earlier fluctuations of fortune and various changes of command, and these were at the very least due for some refresher training. Some of this deficiency, at least, could now be put right, for the desert is, among other things, an ideal training area.

Fifty miles behind the line there were areas where tanks, infantry and artillery could, with maximum realism, rehearse the forthcoming battle on ground that exactly resembled that over which they would have to fight. In conditions as close as possible to actual battle they could practise the intimacies and complications of interservice communication procedures that are the invisible sinews of mechanized warfare; the sinews which make it possible for infantrymen, gunners, sappers, and tank crews to comprehend one another's intentions, capabilities, predicaments, and needs as instinctively as they do their own, and to fight as one integrated army.

The chief focus during this intensive training period was on the recently formed X Armoured Corps which Montgomery had created as his answer to the Afrika Korps, his *corps de chasse.* In its final form it now comprised the 1st and 10th Armoured Divisions and the 2nd New Zealand Division with the 9th (British) Armoured Brigade under its command.

This last combination was in line with a new idea, then being tried out, of changing the structure of the British infantry division (normally three infantry brigades) to two infantry brigades and one armored brigade. The 2nd New Zealand Division had only two infantry brigades anyway, but they were numerically above standard strength and they were fully motorized and therefore well suited to work with the armored corps. This was a formidable force, as the 10th Armoured Division incorporated two armored brigades instead of the usual one, which meant that the corps, with four armored brigades altogether, would field some 700 tanks. These included the 300 new Sherman tanks from America, the best in every way that the British had yet had, made available through the generosity of President Roosevelt: and, to work with the armored divisions, the American self-propelled gun named the Priest—a 105-mm. artillery piece mounted on a tank chassis.

While these powerful forces learned to handle their new equipment and trained under the cold eye of their general—an ordeal in itself, for mistakes were not forgiven at any level, high or low, and weeding out of the inadequate was ruthless— the Alamein line itself, which by now had the institutional air of permanence of the Western Front in that earlier war, was still held by more or less the same infantry divisions on both sides. However, a program of staggered reliefs on the British side made it possible to pull out formations in turn to undergo the same grueling routine as their armored colleagues.

Some distance behind all this there was a different but no less frantic activity as the tanks and guns and trucks and all the rest of the prodigious influx of stores and supplies of all kinds were handled through the Egyptian ports and filtered forward to the bases and dumps from which they would feed the battle to come.

Every single night R.A.F. *Wellington* bombers added to Rommel's already considerable supply difficulties by bombing the shipping and the port installations at Tobruk. While the longer-range *Liberators* (98th Bombardment Group) of General Brereton's U. S. Air Forces in the Middle East, later renamed the U. S. 9th Air Force, did the same to Benghazi and Tripoli. (At this time four squadrons of the U. S. 12th Bombardment Group and three squadrons of the 57th Fighter Group were operating with the R.A.F. under Air Vice-Marshal Coningham's Desert Air Force command.) Montgomery liked making full use of the Royal Air Force, and the R.A.F. responded eagerly to the requirements of a general who seemed to understand so well what an air force can and cannot do.

On the other side of no man's land, where the Panzerarmee Afrika reorganized and adjusted to the near certainty that they would be receiving little in the way of reinforcement or new equipment but would have to make the best of what they had, there was a further blow to their morale when it was learned that Rommel would shortly be leaving. His medical adviser, Professor Dr. Horster, had long been urging a complete rest and proper treatment for his liver and blood pressure conditions. Now Hitler himself had intervened and sent a message ordering him to take sick leave; a replacement,

General Georg Stumme, who had been commanding a corps on the Russian front, would shortly be on his way to take temporary command.

The forthcoming departure of the field-marshal was a considerable disappointment at a time when his army needed all the boost it could get. His hold over the imagination of German and Italian troops alike was by this time so complete that to fight without him was unthinkable: he was at once their chief, their idol, their father-figure, their friend. And in the ashes of this tremendous summer that had begun in such high elation—their one hope. Rommel would get them out of all this. Rommel would think of something. Trust Rommel to pull something out of the bag no matter how many tanks and aircraft were reaching the British Eighth Army.

It is a journalistic cliché to write of officers who are "worshiped" by their men. The word is a fanciful extravagance. The circumstances of war are not conducive to theistic relations between soldiers and their officers. The bond in its extreme form is much more that of youngsters to a parent or elder brother in whom there is total faith that whatever happens he will look after them. There may be in addition a touch of glamour and Rommel undoubtedly had this too—as even his opponents agreed.

It was not the same appeal as that which Montgomery had so far had time to develop for the Eighth Army. The British Army was riven by the same nuances of class distinction that even today still affect British society. The "smart" regiments—the Guards, the cavalry, and certain others—constituted a sort of Establishment within the army. They exerted considerable influence and were inclined to be a little independent. This element by no means accepted Montgomery, the new member of the club, straight off; especially after he had sacked one or two of the officers. They even went so far as to hint that "the little man," as some of them liked to call him, was something of an upstart.

As compared with Rommel's glamour, the initial appeal of Montgomery for most of his army was more Mosaic or Cromwellian in tone: that of an ascetic who would lead the way into battle with a grenade in one hand and a Bible in the other. Later, of course, under the mellowing influence of success, and thanks to some calculated eccentricities and good public relations, the appeal would broaden and gain warmth. For the time being (to change the metaphor) Montgomery rather resembled the tough new managing director who will stop at nothing to make the business pay. The loss of Rommel to his men at this time was more personally felt. But there were two consolations. Rommel did not think that Montgomery would attack for six or eight weeks, by which time he would be back. There was time, before he handed over to his deputy, to complete the defense plan for the coming battle and ensure that the necessary directives were issued.

The essence of the Rommel plan was simple.[1] By stabilizing the front on this 38-mile stretch of desert between the sea and the Qattara Depression, the British had ensured that the decisive battle would have to be a static affair on the 1914–18 pattern. Therefore the mobile defense, making full use of his panzers, that Rommel preferred was out of the question.

Montgomery would have to attack head-on and force a way through fixed defenses—there was no way round. If he broke through he would unloose through the gap the great torrent of tanks that he now possessed. Therefore it followed that he must not be permitted to break through. The policy must therefore be that of Petain at Verdun, *Ils ne passeront pas!* The Panzerarmee Afrika must create a fortress position that would prevent passage. How do you create a fortress position on a flat stretch of desert without the high ground

that is the stuff of military defense? The answer was the mine
—a diabolical and terrifying weapon that was just beginning to
come into its own and was destined to exert a major influence
over the battlefields of the second half of the war. Minefields,
deeper, more intense and more ingeniously devilish than ever
before, must be prepared to delay and frustrate the attacker
and cripple his advance to the main defense belt which would
then destroy him. (It was the strength of the British minefields, remember, that had vitally hindered Rommel's own recent offensive at Alam el Halfa on the first night).

The new German layout was as follows. There was first
the outer minefield for the attackers to traverse and at the far
end of which they would meet the outpost positions. Some of
these section posts were actually inside the minefield and there
would be narrow clear-ways left so that the "suicide squads"
who manned them could get to them.

Beyond this first mine belt it would be up to a mile to the
second and wider belt, at the far end of which (from the
attacker's point of view) the main defenses would be encoun-
tered. These defenses would include the bulk of the infantry
emplacements, dug-in tanks and antitank guns, and would extend back to a depth of 5,000 yards. The entire defense belt,
from outer edge of first minefield to the rear of the main
positions, was to be 5 miles deep along much of the front.
Behind this 5-mile belt would be the tanks in two groups supported by a third line of defenses running south along the
Rahman track. One group of tanks was behind the northern,
one behind the southern sector and so placed that they could
move to any point of the front where a breakthrough was
threatened.

This was the fortress that Rommel ordered built in the
sand, and to man it as effectively as possible he sandwiched
the Italian infantry between the Germans, not only by formations but, where possible, by battalions also, with the respec-

THE PREPARATIONS [69]

tive headquarters near to one another so that the German commander could steel the resolve of his neighbor and, if necessary, take over both units. It was the German view that the weak links in the Italian army of the day were poor equipment and indifferent junior leadership, and that the troops would fight well, especially in well-prepared defenses, if they were properly led.[2]

The sandwiching principle was extended also to the armored divisions. Behind the northern sector of the front the 15th Panzer and Littorio Divisions were paired as the counterattack force, in the south 21st Panzer and Ariete Divisions.

If the British wanted a battle of attrition they could have one. The master of maneuver, confined by the terrain to the kind of static clash that was most alien to his temperament and talent, would make his opponents pay dearly for every yard. But the catch, which perhaps he could not bring himself to admit even to himself, was that Montgomery could afford a battle of attrition, he could not.

Having given all the necessary orders for the defense of the position, Rommel handed over the command to General Stumme and left, on September 23, for the mountain resort of Semmering in Austria.

General Stumme, doubtless gratified by this fortuitous posting to Egyptian sunshine from the oncoming Russian winter, was nevertheless somewhat "put out" (Rommel's words) when the field-marshal remarked, just before leaving, that of course he would come straight back and take over if by any chance Montgomery did happen to start the offensive while he was away.

It was not to be a happy assignment for poor Stumme. He was fifty-six—six years older than Rommel—and a sufferer from high blood pressure, which seems ever to be the occupational complaint of generals regardless of race, creed or color. It was bad enough having to try to assume the mantle of

Rommel in this private army that was as much of a club as the Eighth Army across the wire. To make his task more difficult the army's three senior staff officers were all sick—Gause, the chief of staff, seriously enough to have to be sent home; Westphal with jaundice, and Bayerlein with amoebic dysentery.

(It is worth noting, in passing, that the Eighth had a distinct edge on its opponents in the management of its health. The British Army and its Medical Corps, with long experience of service in eastern and tropical climates, mastered the health problems of the desert without difficulty and it was noticeable that the majority of soldiers actually thrived on the hard but healthy life imposed. Among the German and Italian soldiers, on the other hand, the general level of health and the incidence of dysentery and other local ailments was a constant source of worry to the higher command.)

On his way through Rome, Rommel took the chance to implore Mussolini to galvanize his navy into providing better protection for the supply convoys to Africa. The Duce made a number of promises, but Rommel could feel no confidence that they would amount to anything. Then he visited Hitler and reported at length on recent operations and the great opportunity he considered that Germany was missing by failing to reinforce the African front and maintain it adequately.

Rommel saw more clearly than Hitler and the Supreme Command the possibilities that would be opened up by a victory in Egypt: how it could become the southern jaw of a huge pincer moving through the Middle East to meet the more northerly German thrust into the Caucasus. But he could not persuade Hitler and the rest of them to see it his way. Africa was still to them a sideshow and they thought he exaggerated his difficulties.[3]

He needled Goering by graphically describing the dominance of the Royal Air Force in the recent battle, its devastating new tactics of carpet-bombing, the huge buildup that Montgomery was receiving, and how the influence of America's great industrial war potential was now beginning to be felt. Hitler soothed him with promises of new shallow-draft ferries (that would be less vulnerable to torpedoes) for his supply fleet, and the latest Tiger tanks and a brigade of the new multi-barreled mortar called a *nebelwerfer*. But Rommel knew that none of these could arrive in time, and he had the impression that Hitler and the others did not really care. The desert campaign was only a sideshow. All that really interested them was their coming offensive in Russia about which they were all tremendously optimistic, the one that later in the year would reach Stalingrad.

So when at last he arrived at the little resort of Semmering he felt thoroughly frustrated and furious with them all for not being able to see how much he could achieve for Germany with, as he considered, so little more; and, being the active man he was, the enforced rest that was now his merely gave him more long empty hours in which to brood and worry and fret. It was not a helpful state of mind in which to start a treatment for high blood pressure.

THE PLAN

6   MONTGOMERY claimed that his plan for the battle was a departure from the doctrine of armored warfare then current.[1] According to him it had come to be generally accepted that the aim should be first to destroy the enemy armor and then deal with his infantry. Montgomery proposed to reverse the procedure. This was because he initially felt more confident in his infantry than his tanks. (The Australians and New Zealanders were quite outstanding and great things were expected of the fresh-to-battle 51st Highland Division, reformed since the loss of the first Highland Division at St. Valery, France, in 1940, and keen to avenge its predecessor.)

The main blow was to be delivered in the northern sector of the front by XXX Corps. From north to south 9th Australian, 51st Highland, 2nd New Zealand and 1st South African Divisions would simultaneously attack on a front of six miles between the Tel el Eisa and Miteirya ridges. Further south, 4th Indian Division would at the same time make diversionary raids.

The task of XXX Corps was—in the oversimplified but convenient lingo of higher command—"to punch two corridors through the enemy defenses and minefields." When this had been done X Corps (1st and 10th Armoured Divisions) would pass through these corridors and position themselves defensively to hold off tank counterattacks.

Meanwhile behind this armored screen XXX Corps infantry, wheeling north or south, would proceed to the second task, which was to begin the systematic destruction, by a series of set-piece attacks, of the infantry manning the defenses into which they had just broken. For this intended process of attrition Montgomery had coined the expression "crumbling."

Simultaneously with the main attack in the northern sector by XXX Corps, XIII Corps, which included 7th Armoured Division, would attack the minefields in the southern sector. This was to be a subsidiary attack. Its chief purpose was to keep the enemy guessing as long as possible whether the northern or southern thrust was the main one and, by so doing, ensure that he was contained for the time being in the south, especially his armor in this sector.

If by chance the southern attack succeeded in making a substantial penetration, the infantry of XIII Corps was to set about the enemy infantry while 7th Armoured Division fully exploited any gap that had been made. But this was thought unlikely to happen. XIII Corps would have done its duty if by aggressive activity it kept 21st Panzer Division in the south.

As half a million mines would dominate this battle due to start at 10 o'clock on the night of October 23, the operation was code-named, with macabre flippancy, LIGHTFOOT.

The problem now was to conceal from the enemy the time and place where the main attack was to be made. To achieve this a most elaborate and thorough cover plan was worked out and put into operation more than a month before D-day.[2]

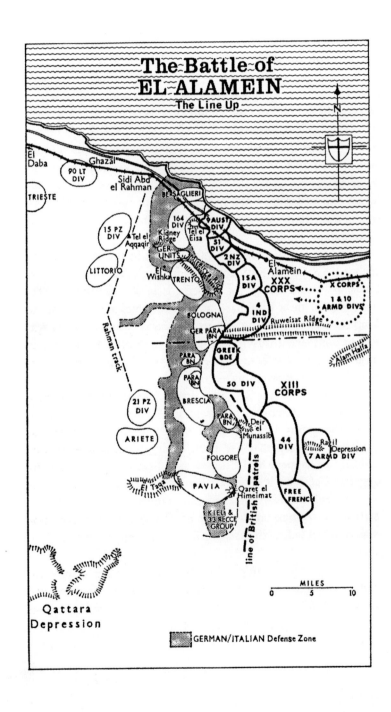

The Battle of
EL-ALAMEIN
The Line Up

N

El Daba

Ghazal

90 LT DIV

Sidi Abd el Rahman

TRIESTE

BERSAGLIERI

164 DIV

AUST DIV

15 PZ DIV

Tel el Aqqaqir

Kidney Ridge

Tel el Eisa

GER. UNITS

51 DIV

El Wishka

2 NZ DIV

El Alamein

LITTORIO

TRENTO

15A DIV

XXX CORPS

X CORPS

1 & 10 ARMD DIVS

Rahman track

BOLOGNA

4 IND DIV

Ruweisat Ridge

GER PARA BN

GREEK BDE

Alam Halfa

PARA BN

PARA BN

50 DIV

XIII CORPS

21 PZ DIV

BRESCIA

PARA BN

Deir el Munassib

ARIETE

44 DIV

Ragil Depression

7 ARMD DIV

FOLGORE

El Taqa

PAVIA

Qaret el Himeimat

line of British patrols

FREE FRENCH

KIEL & 33 RECCE GROUP

MILES

0   5   10

Qattara Depression

GERMAN/ITALIAN Defense Zone

It should be explained that the most eloquent evidence of enemy intentions in any battle zone is the varying density and location of guns, stores, and especially transport. This was particularly so in the open desert where concealment was virtually impossible. The aerial photographs from the daily air reconnaissance carried out by each side provided a running commentary on what the other side was up to and how soon action seemed likely.

The Eighth Army was to open its offensive with an attack by XXX Corps in the northern part of the front on October 23. The aim of the cover plan, therefore, was to indicate to the enemy aerial photographers that the main attack was to be made by XIII Corps in the south: and that it was timed for about two weeks later than the true date. The principle of the plan was to work out what the ground picture of the battle zone would look like just before the battle; then, by means of a centrally controlled pool of transport and large numbers of fabricated dummy trucks, tanks and guns, to maintain this layout from a month beforehand, so that there would be no apparent day-to-day change except where it was deliberately intended to mislead.

In the southern sector, therefore, a buildup of troops and transport would be shown indicative of impending attack. But the administrative preparations also displayed would be left incomplete, thus suggesting that the attack was not coming for some time.

In the northern sector, where a considerable artillery reinforcement of XXX Corps was intended, dummy trucks made of wood and canvas occupied the new gun areas early in October. When the guns and limbers were due to take over the positions they came forward by night and moved straight into concealment under the dummies. In the southern sector, on the other hand, where it was intended to mislead the enemy, the XIII Corps buildup of artillery was flaunted by an early

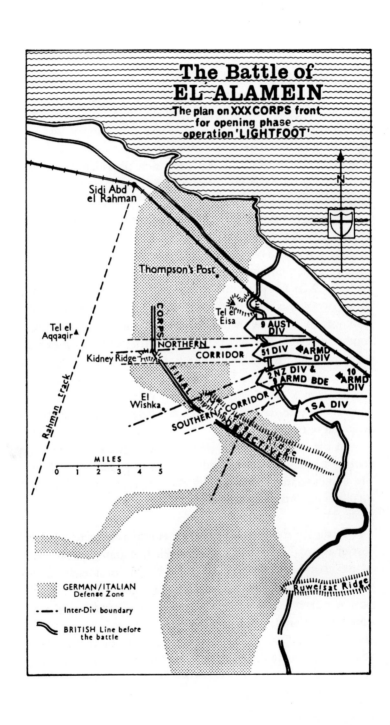

The Battle of EL ALAMEIN
The plan on XXX CORPS front for opening phase operation 'LIGHTFOOT'

N

Sidi Abd el Rahman

Thompson's Post

Tel el Aqqaqir

Rahman track

Kidney Ridge

El Wishka

Tel el Eisa

9 AUST DIV

51 DIV

ARMD DIV

2 NZ DIV & 9 ARMD BDE

10 ARMD DIV

1 SA DIV

CORPS

NORTHERN CORRIDOR

FINAL

SOUTHERN CORRIDOR

OBJECTIVE

Miteiriya Ridge

MILES
0 1 2 3 4 5

GERMAN/ITALIAN Defense Zone

Inter-Div boundary

BRITISH Line before the battle

Ruweisat Ridge

siting of 240 dummy guns—replaced in due course by the real ones.

The forward move of X Corps from its training area 50 miles behind the line was one of the trickiest to manage, as its two armoured divisions had 700 tanks and 4,000 trucks between them. Many of these trucks were already in place among the 4,000 maintained in the assembly areas on the northern front destined to receive these divisions. The move was made in two stages: the first, openly in daylight as if a routine training march, brought them significantly close to the southern sector of the front. The final move north to their real assembly areas was made by night, and, as they moved out of the intermediate staging area, the transport they took with them was replaced, so that no move was apparent. As the corps reached the assembly areas the equivalent of the transport that it brought in was moved out. And 700 dummy trucks that had been in the areas for days were fitted over the incoming 700 tanks. Stores were concealed by camouflage or by stacking them in shapes that would photograph from the air as trucks.

The forward movement of any substantial number of operational vehicles was always made at night so that dummies or other vehicles could take their place. Similar adjustments were made at the destination so that the quota of vehicles at both ends remained constant.

One of the most effective items in this program was a dummy water pipeline. It ran from the main pipeline, which was near the coast, toward the southern sector, and, though made of old gasoline tins, photographed like the real thing from the air. To complete authenticity the pipeline was equipped with reservoirs and pumping stations. But its progress was so timed as to indicate that it would probably not be completed until the first week of November.

These were some of the artifices intended to deceive not only the aerial photographers but also Rommel's observers on

Himeimat—the high ground Montgomery had not been un-happy to leave in Panzerarmee Afrika's possession after the battle of Alam el Halfa.

The cover plan achieved some success. As late as October 20 the enemy commander, Stumme, could issue a directive no more specific than to be prepared for an attack at any time from any direction, and in the event it was not until D plus 3 (according to the Alexander *Despatch*) that opposition devel-oped its full strength against the main Eighth Army attack. On the other hand it is well established that the un-Rommel-like dispersion of the Axis armor between north and south ordered by Rommel before he went away, was in fact due not to the British deception plan but to the Axis need to conserve its gasoline. The enemy could not, initially, allow his armored divisions the luxury of unlimited mobility.

The comparative strengths of the two armies on the eve of the battle showed a manpower superiority of 3 to 1 in favor of the Eighth Army with 230,000 fighting troops to the ene-my's 77,000, of which 27,000 were German. Montgomery had 1,400 tanks ready for action (480 of them Shermans or Grants) as compared with 500 (200 of them German)—an effective superiority of 6 to 1 if the inferior Italian tanks are discounted. The Eighth Army had another 1,000 tanks in Egypt—but not another 1,000 battle-trained tank crews, a fac-tor to be borne in mind when considering gross figures of tank reserves. In field and medium artillery, with 892 British pieces opposing 552, the balance was less favorable to the attackers, and in antitank guns the Panzerarmee was strongly placed for static defense with 1,000 to the Eighth Army's 1,450. In the air Montgomery had 880 serviceable aircraft (including 100 American) available to support him from bases in Egypt and Palestine as compared with the 129 German and 216 Italian planes available to his opponents. And of course the Royal

Navy continued to dominate the waters through which the Panzerarmee's supplies had to come.

In considering Montgomery's seemingly unbeatable superiority in "fighting troops" it is essential to realize that a vast proportion of them were solely engaged in keeping the comparatively few actual assault infantry, engineers, gunners and tank crews in action: maintaining, in the featureless, trackless, waterless desert, the prodigious supply of ammunition, gasoline, food, water, spare parts, and mechanical services required at the front day and night. In such circumstances "fighting troops" is a relative term.

Thus events moved to their climax: a climax for which the moral preparation had been as carefully controlled and built up by Montgomery as the tactical. In every way this was a "production."

On September 14 Montgomery issued orders concerning morale:

This battle for which we are preparing will be a real rough house and will involve a very great deal of hard fighting. If we are successful it will mean the end of the war in North Africa. . . . Morale is the big thing in war. . . . This battle may go on for many days and the final issue may well depend on which side can best last out and stand up to the buffeting, the ups and downs, and the continuous strain of hard battle fighting.

I am not convinced that our soldiery are really tough and hard. . . . During the next months, therefore, it is essential to make our officers and men really fit; ordinary fitness is not enough, they must be made tough and hard.[3]

On October 6 he issued orders about leadership:

This battle will involve hard and prolonged fighting. Our troops must not think that, because we have a good tank and very powerful artillery support, the enemy will all surrender. The enemy will *not* surrender, and there will be bitter fighting. The infantry must be prepared to fight and kill, and to continue doing so over a prolonged period. . . .

There have been far too many unwounded prisoners taken in this war. We must impress on our officers, N.C.O.'s and men that when they are cut off or surrounded, and there appears to be no hope of survival, they must organise themselves into a defensive locality and hold out where they are. . . .[4]

The unveiling of the plan was meticulously controlled. Briefings, beginning at the top and radiating down the chain of command and outwards, began on September 28 when brigadiers and commanders of the all-important Royal Engineer units were let into the secret. On October 10 other unit commanders were told. A week after that the commanders were allowed to pass it on to their subordinates, the company, squadron or battery commanders.

Only on October 21, two days before the battle, were these commanders in their turn allowed to brief their junior officers, NCOs and men. This insistence, by Montgomery, that every man should go into battle knowing exactly what the plan was and exactly what he personally had to do was one of the most important features of his doctrine of leadership. Considered in retrospect it might seem so obvious as hardly to merit mention. But soldiers who have known active service will have little difficulty in recalling the number of occasions on which they were plunged into battle with only the sketchiest notion of what was supposed to happen and no orders more explicit than the worried and breathless "Follow me!" of an equally baffled senior officer. This must always be remembered in any assessment of Montgomery. He was always most insistent about everyone being "in the picture."

Consciously or unconsciously all this helped to create and sustain tension, like a carefully constructed drama. When, on the morning of October 23, the army read, or heard read, his special order of the day, with its facile cricket metaphor and somewhat corny invocation of "the Lord mighty in battle," the words nevertheless seemed appropriate enough to the calculated mood: the very last stage of a process of dramatic logic leading inexorably to a moment of history.

The prologue duly spoken, the curtain could now rise.

THE NIGHT OF GUNS
AND MINES

7   IT BEGAN IN bright moonlight at 2140 hours on October 23 with a shattering bombardment of every known enemy gun position by the entire Eighth Army artillery—just under 900 guns. The shelling continued with maximum intensity for fifteen minutes in an effort to cripple the enemy artillery before the main proceedings opened.[1]

It was the most spectacular artillery effort yet seen in the campaign and it impressed both sides. For the rest of the war "Alamein barrage" became a term of convenience in the British Army to describe any artillery plan that was intended to sound impressive.

Under cover of this barrage, gladdened by its noise, excited by the demonic beauty of the dancing flashes behind them, heartened by its magisterial fracture of the long pre-battle tension, the infantry of XXX Corps moved up to their start line in no man's land for the attack—a line identified and marked for them with tape by their unit reconnaissance parties the night before.

At 2155 the guns paused for five minutes as the infantry arranged themselves in the final extended formation in which they would attack. Then at 2200—H-hour for the attack—the guns resumed firing, but this time on the enemy's forward positions. The opening of this new bombardment, which would continue for the rest of the night, was the signal for the assault wave of infantry to advance across no man's land to the first minefield and its covering outposts—in most cases a mile and a half away.

From now on the XXX Corps, whose four infantry divisions were making the main effort, would have 474 guns in immediate support for a night's work that was supposed to take them through the enemy's main defense line. It was a hard program for one night, with a final objective stretching from two miles north of Kidney Ridge to the northern tip of Miteirya Ridge and thence southeast along its full length—the New Zealanders and South Africans each taking three miles of it. This meant that the Australians and the Highlanders, who had the farthest to go, would have to cover 5 miles from their start line.

To clarify its design the attack was to be in two phases, with an intermediate objective line behind the first defense belt. The corps had till midnight to clear this. Then the men had a pause of an hour to reorganize and sort themselves out before getting on the move again at 0100 hours with their second assault wave. They were scheduled to reach the final objective line—through the main defenses—by 0245 hours, i.e., in less than two hours.

In the three remaining hours before daylight they were to consolidate, while the tanks of X Corps, having crossed the same start line at 0200 hours, and making their own gaps in the minefields as they advanced, caught up the infantry, and pushing out through the bridgehead, formed an iron buffer a mile or two beyond.

As soon as the attack had started, the codeword ZIP was

signaled to Prime Minister Churchill in London who informed President Roosevelt:

The battle in Egypt began tonight at 8 P.M. London time. The whole force of the army will be engaged. I will keep you informed. A victory there will be most fruitful to our main enterprise. All the Shermans and self-propelled guns which you gave me on that dark Tobruk morning will play their part.[2]

In his diary the Chief of the General Staff, General Brooke, Montgomery's staunch champion in London, wrote: "This evening after dinner received call from War Office to say that Middle East attack had started. We are bound to have some desperately anxious moments. . . . If it fails I don't quite know how I shall bear it."[3] And years later he was to write: "I remember that evening as if it was yesterday, and can see myself sitting at my writing-table in my Westminster Gardens flat, finishing those last lines and remaining staring into space."

The man who seemed least concerned was General Montgomery. For him ten o'clock was not only H-hour for the second battle of Alamein but his usual bedtime in or out of battle. As soon as he knew the attack was on its way he went to bed. Everything possible had been arranged. There was nothing more he could do. The battle must take its course and he must wake up fresh to meet the problems and decisions of the next day.

The infantry stepped off in extended line, two or three yards between each man. Because this was Egypt they wore tropical khaki shirts and shorts, but because it was night they wore over their shirts the woollen cardigans that had become the night uniform of the desert. They carried their rifles at the high port with bayonets fixed. On their backs in a small pack high on their shoulders they carried what for the next few days would be their entire worldly wealth and biscuits and bully beef that would have to sustain them for at least 24 hours. A proportion of them carried Bren guns or light mortars. Everyone carried grenades and sandbags they could fill for their protection if the ground was too rocky to dig. The pattern was the same in all the divisions.

Because this was the desert and there were no landmarks, just to keep direction was appallingly difficult and each battalion assault wave was led by a navigating officer who marched a little way ahead, compass in hand and counting the paces, while a drum of tape was unrolled behind him so that those who came after would have a guiding line to the center of battalion. It was lonely and perilous to be a navigating officer that night, and one battalion had seven of them killed or wounded during the night.

The fire of the artillery was perhaps the most reliable guide to position when the navigating officers were in difficulty. Surveyed into their positions the gunners could fire accurately on named targets which the infantry had marked on their gridded maps. Further to assist them it was arranged that each division's light antiaircraft guns should fire tracers to mark the brigade and divisional boundaries. Crossed searchlights intersecting above the objective were also tried, though this idea did not prove a success.

Behind the leading infantry followed groups of engineers with the dangerous task of gapping the minefields. Putting into practice the new drills that had been specially devised and rehearsed for this battle in which mines were to figure so predominantly, each team divided into small groups of two or three. One group would find the mines with the new Polish electronic detectors, a second would mark with tape the lane to be cleared, the third would secure the tape to the ground. Then they would return through the lane on their knees, carefully lifting the mines but first feeling delicately around with their fingers for wires that would indicate that the mines were booby-trapped. If they found one that was, the officer or

NCO in charge looped signal cable round it, withdrew to a safe distance, and when everyone was lying flat, exploded it with a sharp pull. The other mines were immobilized and stacked and the team moved on.

Another team would then check the lane and at the same time mark it more clearly with a single strand of wire looped to small pickets along each side, and small hooded lamps were affixed to the pickets as well.

The new Polish mine detector (invented by a Polish officer serving in Britain) was making its debut in this battle, 500 of them having been rushed out to Eighth Army in time for Alamein, but some were faulty and many became damaged in action, so that a great deal of the mine-detecting in the battle had still to be done in the old way—by men crawling forward on their knees while delicately prodding with bayonets. This was a more dangerous procedure, much slower, and required twice as many men.

There were two principal types of German mines in use at this time, the Teller and the S. The Teller antitank mine was a large flat canister which took the weight of a vehicle to explode. The S-mine was the one the marching men had to beware of. It was a small round canister about the size of a cigarette tin. When set for action nothing showed above the ground but three small wire prongs. If these were trodden on, the mine jumped out of the ground and exploded high enough to discharge its lethal fragments into any part of the body.

As the antitank mines were the ones that were then being used in the largest numbers, the infantry were expected to take their chance. The serious mine-lifting then took place to clear the lanes for the infantry's follow-up vehicles bringing their supporting arms and further supplies of ammunition. The marching men were expected to keep marching. But no one would blame them if, with the corner of their eyes, they watched keenly for three little wire prongs that in the bright moonlight they might be lucky enough to spot before a foot came down on the mine.

The pattern was the same in each of these divisions which talked and joked and cursed in the same English language but with different accents. The companies of the 51st Highland Division of Scotland were led not only by their officers but by their pipers.

There is something incongruous and magnificently tribal about the pipers of Scottish regiments piping the riflemen into battle in the most mechanized of modern wars. The pipers were vulnerable targets and several were killed. There was no more poignantly bizarre symbol of Alamein than the young piper of the Black Watch lying mortally wounded, hugging to the last his preposterous bagpipes. The Australians on the right and the New Zealanders on the left occasionally caught distant snatches of the music when the guns were momentarily stilled and they were not unmoved.

The first objective line was reached by all four divisions on time or soon after and without much difficulty. There was time to reorganize and brace themselves for the second phase of the attack which was certain to be more difficult, for they would now meet the main enemy defenses.

At 0100 hours the advance was resumed and the main battle opened, the companies that had followed in reserve the first time themselves now leading. To begin with, three of the divisions advanced close behind a creeping barrage, but the Australian commander, Major-General L. J. (later Sir Leslie) Morshead, preferred the more specific method of support for his attack by heavy artillery concentrations on known enemy strongpoints and on targets that arose as his division progressed. One o'clock in the morning is not a congenial time at which to go into the attack; but, on the other hand, it is not an agreeable hour at which to crouch in a machine-gun pit at the receiving end of a barrage while waiting for men with bayonets and grenades to spring out of the dust fog created by the bursting shells. It was to be a crucifying night for everyone.

As anticipated, the opposition was now much stronger. The leading companies were soon in heavy trouble, and the night began to resolve itself into scores of apparently unrelated tiny battles between sections and platoons and isolated posts: five men against two with a machine gun; two platoons against a wired and reinforced strongpoint; six men desperately trying to extinguish the flames of a blazing ammunition truck lighting up the night and attracting a storm of enemy fire—a confusion of fragments that only later would be seen to make up a battle mosaic with its own form and momentum.

The attack quickly turned into a nightmare of confusion in which no group knew where it was or where anyone else was. The barrage had churned up the whole area into a great bank of dust, thickened by the sour smoke of the bursting shells and mortar bombs, and hugely aggravated by every vehicle that moved forward or back with stores, ammunition or wounded. Visibility was down to a few yards in spite of the bright moonlight. And worse was to come, for the armored divisions of Lieutenant-General Herbert Lumsden's X Corps were now following close behind, preceded by their own mine-lifting task forces striving to clear a way for the tanks. Altogether there were four armored brigades numbering 700 tanks crawling forward behind the sappers.

The organized chaos, as soldiers call it, became worse as the night wore on, and the dust thickened into choking suffocating permanency. Major-General R. M. P. Carver, who was a lieutenant-colonel on the staff of 7th Armoured Division at the time, has vividly described it:

There were masses of vehicles all over the place and the marking of routes and gaps was very hard to see. It needed only a vehicle or two to stray off the side to remove all the signs and lead everybody behind into confusion. Tempers got as heated as the engines while the tanks and other vehicles ground along at snail's pace in the billowing clouds of dust. . . . The whole area looked like a badly organised car park at an immense race meeting held in a dust bowl.⁴

The infantry had long since forgotten the grand design with its persuasive diagrammatic talk of corridors through the enemy defenses for the tanks to pass through. They could only stumble on through the choking fog; praying that they were going in the right direction; striving desperately to keep some semblance of contact with those on their right and left— if only to have the negative reassurance that these others too had little idea of where they were or of what was happening. It was the time when the battle in its confusion belongs to the company and platoon commanders and to the artillery observers.

The job of the infantry was to keep moving through the dust, attacking anyone who tried to stop them; moving forward, no matter how many of them fell wounded or dead; stumbling, walking, running on through the blinding, choking dust to the end of the night, praying that if and when they got there it would be the right place.

Meanwhile the sappers, who at least had something clear-cut and useful to do, patiently concentrated on their nerve-wracking skilled task; sweeping the ground with their mine detectors in the incongruous rhythm of housewives; probing with bayonets, feeling with delicate pickpocket fingers round the submerged canisters for the wires that would proclaim a booby trap, and, if there were none, lifting them with relief, but as tenderly as if they were precious porcelain, mine after mine to be rendered harmless; then replacing the marking tape and the wire and hooded guide lamps that vehicles, slithering in the loose sand, and bursting shells kept deranging.

Behind came the tank crews, choking and sweating in

their overheated clattering machines, fretted because it was all so appallingly slow and the night was passing so swiftly that it seemed they could never be clear of the minefields before daybreak. For those with the task of joining the infantry on the objective at dawn (to help them stay there) the night is never long enough. This one was no exception.

By daybreak on October 24 the XXX Corps had made a sizable dent in the enemy front, but the passing through of the armored divisions of X Corps had not been accomplished. This was the position from right to left. The Australian Division on the far right had captured most of its share of the final objective. The Highlanders were 1,500 yards short of their final objective and were held up by strongpoints in what should have been the northern corridor. This meant that 1st Armoured Division, which by now should have passed along this corridor through the minefields and the infantry bridgehead into the open, was in fact still bogged down in the minefields about 2 miles back.

The 2nd New Zealand Division with its British 9th Armoured Brigade had reached its final objective, Miteirya Ridge, as day was breaking. 10th Armoured Division was just behind, emerging from the southern corridor, which had been cleared in time. But attempts by the tanks to exploit beyond the ridge were frustrated by a new minefield on its crest and by enemy guns which were subjecting the ridge to a murderous defensive fire that forced the tanks to remain hull-down on the near side.

Farther to the left the 1st South African Division was 500 yards short of the ridge, which was its final objective also. The night's casualties gave some indication of where the main opposition had been. The Australians and the South Africans had had 350 casualties each, the New Zealanders 800, the Highland Division 1,000. XXX Corps had about 1,000 prisoners to show for the night's work.

On the southern part of the front in the supporting attack by Lieutenant-General B. G. (later Sir Brian) Horrocks's XIII Corps, 7th Armoured Division breached the first enemy minefield but not the second, and an infantry attack on Himeimat also failed.

General Montgomery was dissatisfied with the gains that had been made, and at his morning conference with the corps commanders he ordered General Leese to give first priority to completing the clearance of the northern corridor, and General Lumsden to give explicit instructions to his armored divisions that they must push on regardless of whether the infantry paved the way or not. It was a reiteration of what Montgomery had made clear before the battle; namely, that the armor must be prepared to fight its own way out of the minefields if necessary. This was not a popular notion with the tank generals, who were apt to take the line that this was not the right way to use tanks—and a long-latent conflict seemed about to come to a head.

While Montgomery's staff was straightening out the picture of the first night's progress and Montgomery himself was clarifying his thoughts on what he wished his corps commanders to do next to complete satisfactorily this opening phase of the operation, a certain chaos was hampering the direction of activities on the other side.

To begin with, Eighth Army's artillery spree the night before had soon shattered the Panzerarmee Afrika's communications network. So General Stumme and his staff had spent the rest of a sleepless night trying desperately to find out what was going on. All that was certain was that they were being attacked at points along the whole 38-mile front and the attacks were being supported by the most prodigious artillery concentrations yet experienced in the desert. Soon after dawn Stumme decided to go forward and find out what was happening. He summoned his driver and a staff colonel named Buechting who was to go with him. His chief of staff advised him to take the usual wireless truck and armored escort, but he refused, saying that he was going no farther than the 90th Light Division (which was in a reserve position some way behind the front). Perhaps, too, he was anxious to make some sort of gesture in front of his staff, who were mostly Rommel men. Anyway, the car departed, but instead of calling on 90th Light Division, Stumme went straight on to the front and as the car approached ground recently taken by the Australians it was fired on. Colonel Buechting was hit in the head and mortally wounded; the corporal-driver whirled the car round and drove off at top speed, his action coinciding with the moment chosen by General Stumme to jump for cover. Poor Stumme, caught half in and half out of the car, hung on as long as he could. His high blood pressure, to which attention has already been drawn, proved unequal to the effort and he fell to a dusty death—not from an Australian bullet but from a heart attack. The result was that Panzerarmee Afrika headquarters learned nothing and lost their general in the process. As it was some time before Stumme's fate became known, it was therefore some time before his place was taken by General von Thoma, commander of the Afrika Korps. They now had the further disruption of General Ritter von Thoma having to take over command of the army after handing over the Afrika Korps to his deputy. It was, from the Axis point of view, a confused and difficult beginning. How long this further disruption of the Panzerarmee Afrika lasted is shown by the fact that it was almost noon before Rommel, still a sick man, received a top priority telephone call at his hotel in Semmering. It was Hitler in the unusual role of a man begging a favor.

"Rommel," said Hitler, "the news from Africa sounds bad. The situation seems somewhat obscure. Nobody appears to know what has happened to General Stumme. Do you feel capable of returning to Africa and taking command of the army again?"⁵ Rommel said that he would leave at once.

Meanwhile Montgomery's firm orders took effect at 1500 hours that afternoon when the 51st Highland and the 1st Armoured Divisions attacked together and completed the clearance of the northern corridor, permitting the armored division to send its armored brigade forward to receive, and indeed to provoke, the counterattacks by which it was intended that the Axis armor should wear itself out.

It was a difficult battle, with divisions of different corps fighting over the same ground, a situation which is bound to lead to some confusion of staff control, transport movement, and supply organization. Map reading and ground identification caused further difficulty in this desert terrain, units being apt to claim that they had taken objectives, and then have these claims disputed by other units. As questioning an officer's map reading is equivalent to an attack on his honor—especially if it is another unit that is raising the doubt—there were many testy arguments about where soldiers were or thought they were. These arguments were to become a notable feature of El Alamein—not because of poor training but simply because of the sheer difficulty of orientation on ground so devoid of identifiable landmarks; ground, moreover, now permanently shrouded in a pall of dust and continually being churned into new surface shapes by swirling, skidding vehicles.

It is an indication of the intensity of the fighting in this afternoon battle that one assault company of the 51st Highland Division reached its objective under the command of the company clerk, all the officers and the sergeant major having been killed or wounded. Meanwhile the South Africans during the day had pushed on to their final objective and the Australians had tidied up some unfinished business on their front. The infantry bridgehead was now virtually complete and by late afternoon the 1st Armoured Division had passed through the northern corridor and taken up positions beyond as it was meant to do.

On the left, however, the 10th Armoured Division had not succeeded in doing the same, but had spent the day, along with the New Zealand Division tanks, engaged in long-range shooting exchanges from the near side of Miteirya Ridge. X Corps had therefore completed only half its task. This was to lead, during the second night of the battle, to the first grave crisis, and thereby to the first crucial test of General Montgomery as a battle commander.

Throughout the day the Desert Air Force (1,000 sorties) and the United States Air Force (147 sorties) had established complete mastery of the air. They repeatedly attacked the Axis forward airfields, tank and vehicle concentrations, troops and gun positions and prevented the enemy air forces from interfering in the battle. Some of the most skillfully concealed enemy gun emplacements were detected and later destroyed by the ground forces because of having to point their barrels upward to resist the ceaseless attacks of British bombers and fighter-bombers.

In the late afternoon 1st Armoured Division, newly emerged from the northern corridor and deployed in defensive positions, was counterattacked by about 100 tanks of the 15th Panzer and Littorio Divisions. This was a favorite time of the panzers to stage a counterattack—they could advance with the blinding glare of the setting sun behind them and full in the eyes of their opponents.

The 1st Armoured Division, established on ground it had chosen, was ready for them. In this first tank engagement of Alamein the panzers met the Sherman tank for the first time and they learned then that the Eighth Army's new tanks were not only superior in number but equal to their own best in quality. The engagement lasted until dusk, when Panzerarmee Afrika withdrew leaving behind about two dozen tanks. The

Eighth had incurred similar losses—but could afford them. This was the prototype of the kind of engagement the British plan had envisaged, with the Panzerarmee wearing itself out on the tanks the Eighth Army had pushed into the Axis defenses —though as yet not deeply enough. The pity was that the 10th Armoured Division had not managed to break out of the southern corridor. Montgomery was determined that it should do so that night.

In his *Memoirs* he has summarized his thoughts and feelings on the morning of October 24 when his armored divisions had failed to get beyond the minefields:

> In accordance with my orders I expected the armoured divisions to fight their way out into the open. But there was some reluctance to do so and I gained the impression during the morning that they were pursuing a policy of inactivity. There was not that eagerness on the part of senior commanders to push on and there was a fear of tank casualties. . . . I therefore sent for Lumsden and told him he must "drive" his divisional commanders, and if there was any more hanging back I would remove them. . . .[6]

This action, according to Montgomery, produced immediate results and by late afternoon the 1st Armoured Division had forced its way beyond the minefields, where, as we have seen, it successfully frustrated the enemy's first armored counterstroke.

It was in a steely mood, therefore, that Montgomery went to bed that night confident that his armored commanders could surely no longer have the least doubt about what was wanted. Yet, according to General Carver, the New Zealand Division commander, General Bernard C. Freyberg, was telephoning his own corps commander, General Oliver W. H. Leese, to express doubts whether the 10th Armoured Division was "properly set up for the attack." And General Leese, talking about this to his fellow corps commander Lumsden, gained

the impression that Lumsden had no confidence in the operation either; and that these doubts (General Carver continues)
were duly passed on to Major-General Francis (later Sir Francis) de Guingand, Montgomery's chief of staff.[7]

This was an ominous atmosphere in which to begin an
operation, and the advance, timed to begin at 2200 hours, got
off to a late start attended by various misfortunes. A minefield-
gapping party was withdrawn in error on a false report that an
enemy attack was imminent. The minefield was more extensive
than anticipated, and though four gaps two tanks wide had
been intended, only two were completed. A bombing attack
by a small number of enemy aircraft managed to hit a column
of gasoline and ammunition trucks and within seconds twenty-
two trucks were blazing and continued to do so for the rest of
the night. The enemy at once knew what was happening. The
fire gave the enemy gunners an admirable mark on which to
range. They stepped up their shelling of the area where the
minefield-gapping parties were working and in which the
tanks were painfully crawling along the just-cleared lanes nose
to tail and two abreast. At 0130 hours the commander of the
leading armored brigade—hampered by the minefields, the
shelling, the confusion caused by the blazing trucks, and by
heavy casualties—requested permission to withdraw behind
Miteirya, believing he might lose all his tanks and achieve
nothing. The commander of 10th Armoured Division (Major-
General A. H. Gatehouse) passed the request to his corps commander (Lumsden) recommending that permission to withdraw be granted. Lumsden telephoned the chief of staff (de
Guingand), explained the position, and said that he agreed
with Gatehouse that the operation should be called off. De
Guingand decided that this was one of the rare occasions when
Montgomery must be awakened to pass judgment, and asked
the two corps commanders to attend a conference in two
hours' time.[8]

It was a conference charged with high drama. The two corps commanders reported at Army Headquarters at 0330 —Leese, the genial burly red-faced Guards officer; Lumsden the good-looking cavalryman with the spare long-legged figure of a man to whom cavalry meant horses before it meant tanks. It was no secret that Lumsden had been critical of Montgomery's plan for X Corps from the time it was first disclosed and had not been too discreet about letting this be known. Freyberg was one who had not kept to himself the thought that "the tanks won't do it." Montgomery was not a man who liked his orders or plans to be regarded as a basis for discussion. He had one of his own jargon words for it. He called it belly-aching and he had announced early in his time with the Eighth Army that he would not tolerate it. Nevertheless he knew that certain senior tank commanders had been critical of the plan, which they thought to be "using tanks wrongly."

He received them in his trailer, while seated on a stool studying a map—which is about the only way an army commander of medium stature can suitably receive two tall lieutenant-generals whose situation in these circumstances is comparable to that of schoolboys summoned by their headmaster. According to de Guingand he listened intently to what each had to say about the current battle—including Lumsden's opinion that the armor had been given an impossible task. Then he saw Lumsden alone and said the tanks could and *would* go through. De Guingand noted that he greeted the generals cheerfully; said what he had to say very quietly but very firmly.

At this bleak four-o'clock-in-the-morning crisis when his offensive was beginning to falter, Montgomery accepted the challenge of high command and the cost in lives that it must sometimes entail. In the total context of the desert campaign this was also, perhaps, the crucial showdown between the roundhead general and the cavaliers under his command.

Both brigades of the 10th Armoured Division continued the difficult advance forward from Miteirya Ridge—the 24th Brigade on the right, the 8th Brigade (whose difficulties had brought on the dramatic crisis just resolved) on the left. Montgomery had agreed to one modification of the existing orders—the 8th Brigade was authorized to continue the advance with one regiment only. At first light this unit, having dealt with a number of posts and rounded up and sent back prisoners, was badly shot up by an antitank gun screen—losing ten tanks in as many seconds. But the 24th Brigade, which knew nothing of the night's drama and had been inching its way through the minefields behind its gapping parties, was clear of them by shortly before 0500 hours. The brigade then pushed 1,000 yards forward of the ridge and managed to establish contact with the 1st Armoured Division on its right.

On the far left, beyond the unlucky 8th Brigade, the 9th Armoured Brigade, under command of the New Zealand Division, had been participating in one of the so-called crumbling attacks by the infantrymen southward against the flank of the salient created by their own penetration of the night before. The infantry attack had met stiff opposition during the night and had been blocked, but the 9th Armoured Brigade had ended the night well forward of the southwestern end of the now notorious Miteirya Ridge, and could oppose any armored counterattacks from that quarter.

So, although the front was not quite so tidy as the official despatch and Montgomery's own account suggest, the break-in—the first phase of Operation LIGHTFOOT—had been completed, but 24 hours behind schedule. The armored screen, not quite complete but in substantial strength, was now in a protective arc beyond the minefields, in positions where it could take on any attempts by the enemy armor to interfere with the infantry's next activities. The infantry could now carry on with the job of exploiting their break-in to the enemy defenses by attacks against the flanks created by their penetrations—as the New Zealanders were already doing, though without positive success beyond the fact that they were wearing the enemy out.

BATTLE OF ATTRITION

8   ON THE MORNING of October 25, the third day of the battle and, as it happened, a Sunday, Montgomery and Middle East Commander-in-Chief Alexander could feel reasonably satisfied with how things were going. XXX Corps had blasted a gap 6 miles wide and 5 miles deep into the strongest part of the enemy mine belt. A total of five armored brigades were now out in front of this gap trying to provoke the counterattacks which they were well placed to smash.

The counterattacks began soon after dawn. They were made by the 15th Panzer and Littorio Divisions, and were directed against the northern corridor, as Eighth Army had hoped. The attacks were not made in strength—groups of between thirty and forty tanks being used. These were accompanied by infantry and by screens of antitank guns—much as a naval task force has its destroyer screen.

The enemy used the familiar tactics perfected during the campaign by the Afrika Korps. They moved forward very slowly, feeling for the curvature and swell of the ground as carefully as infantrymen crawling forward on their bellies, and tried to entice the British to make Balaclava charges in mass for their antitank guns to smash. Especially, they banked on their much feared 88-mm. dual-purpose (antitank or antiaircraft) guns for which the British tank crews had developed an obsessive, almost hypnotic dread. But the British were not to be enticed as they had been in the past. With the 75-mm. guns of their Shermans they could tackle the enemy antitank gun crews at long range with high-explosive shells and then engage the tanks with armor-piercing shot.

In addition to having to run the gauntlet of the well-sited British armored divisions, the panzers had to withstand repeated attacks by Royal Air Force bombers and fighters and the full weight of the artillery of both the armored and the infantry divisions.

These enemy armored counterattacks continued piecemeal throughout the day, but suffered severe losses which they could ill afford, and failed because of the positioning of the British armor—something that had worked out entirely as Montgomery had intended. By nightfall the German 15th Panzer Division had only 31 out of 119 tanks serviceable, though many of the damaged tanks could be recovered and repaired. The 21st Panzer and Ariete Divisions, which could have added weight to these counterattacks, were still immobilized in the southern sector of the front, kept there partly by the threat posed by the XIII Corps and its 7th Armoured Division, but also by the necessity of the Panzerarmee Afrika to conserve its gasoline.

It was now time for the next stage. The initial plan had intended in its second phase that the XXX Corps infantry should attack the north and south flanks of the newly created bulge, thus widening it and in the process destroying the enemy infantry. General Freyberg's New Zealand Division had started to do this the night before by exploiting the southwest flank from Miteirya Ridge. But it had run into strong opposition and suffered heavy losses without achieving much. Though it had fought hard there was a danger (with only two infantry brigades to call on instead of the usual three) that the division might be more crumbled than crumbling. Accordingly about midday on October 25, after conferring with General Freyberg about the way things were going, Montgomery decided to stop the New Zealand Division's move to break through to the southwest and to switch the focus of crumbling to the northern end of the front with an attack northward that night by General Morshead's 9th Australian Division.

This switch was likely to come as a surprise to the enemy, and, in addition, the 5-mile penetration of the Australians in the first 24 hours had provided them with a 5-mile flank that should be well worth a good crumble. It would also give the Australians an opportunity to capture some important hillocks overlooking them from just south of the railway and coast road. It was on one of these, Point 29, that the attack was to be directed.

That afternoon Rommel arrived back at Panzerarmee Afrika Headquarters, having left Austria that morning. He had made his usual brief stop in Rome to learn the latest news. What he heard made him again try to prod the Italian High Command and the attached German Army Commission into getting more gasoline to Africa. He urged them to commandeer every possible U-boat for this purpose, since the Italian navy was seemingly incapable of convoying tankers safely through the British naval and aerial blockade.

His army was more than pleased to have him back and he was brought up to date by Acting Army Commander von Thoma and by Westphal, the chief of staff, who could not offer him much cheer. Gasoline, as always, seemed to be the gloomiest item on the agenda. They were down to three daily issues (an issue being the amount required to move the army 100 kilometers).[1] In consequence counterattacks so far had had to be limited to operations by armored groups against threats to their own part of the front. Rommel decided that the Panzerarmee must concentrate on blocking any further advance by the Eighth Army and driving it out of the parts of his line which it had captured. There was not much else he could decide.

The Australian attack on the night of October 25 was not only a success but was achieved with great panache. The battalion entrusted with the final 2,000-yard assault on Point 29 carried out the assignment with a dashing lack of convention. Halfway to the objective there was a minefield they would have to cross. This was seized as an intermediate objective by two companies who held it while sappers gapped it.

Then the assault company, packed into Bren carriers, raced through the gaps and, charging four carriers abreast, covered the last 1,000 yards in 9 minutes and were right among a completely surprised enemy with the bayonet. In some of the fiercest hand-to-hand fighting of the battle the Australians inflicted 300 casualties on the predominantly German defenders and took more than 200 prisoners. This clear-cut success secured the northern flank of the XXX Corps salient, for the high ground they had captured was one of the rare dominating heights in the area, overlooking the road and railway and linking up with the neighboring ridge of Tel el Eisa. It would play a key part in any further exploitation against the considerable forces now caught in the salient. A new line of exploitation had been opened up.

Concurrently with the Australian attack the 51st Highland Division was required to make progress in the Kidney Ridge area and the 1st Armoured Division to exploit any progress

made. There was none. During the night, however, the South
Africans and the New Zealanders did manage to make their
holdings forward of Miteirya Ridge more secure by means of
a small advance. But it was the Australians' night, and their
success in the north—with its possible future development—
was the news that heartened the Eighth Army Command
when they heard about it.

The next day, October 26, Montgomery withdrew to his
house trailer to consider the situation in solitude. It was one of
his great qualities as a general that he could detach himself in
this way from the fury of a battle and think over his problems
in calm isolation. Undoubtedly he was greatly helped in this
by his deep religious conviction and the genuine comfort and
inspiration he derived from his Bible reading. His house trailer,
which became the holy of holies of his headquarters, was also
something akin to a monk's cell in which maps and meditation
had come to terms. It was undoubtedly one of the unmistakable signs of his greatness as a commander that he had the self-
confidence, coolness, and nerve to be able to detach himself in
this way, completely trusting his chosen subordinates to carry
on. This was one of the reasons why some of the chosen
subordinates developed in the course of time a regard for him
barely this side of idolatry. But, above all, this was why he
never seemed rattled or even worried.

As he thought about the situation on this fourth day of
the battle it seemed clear that the momentum of the offensive
was slowing down and needed a new creative impetus. The
initial attack by XXX and X Corps had taken a great bite out
of the enemy line, and all attempts to recover any of this
ground had been repulsed with crippling losses to the Panzerarmee Afrika. But the enemy had by now succeeded in con-
taining the bridgehead, and by the extreme depth of their
defenses had prevented Eighth Army from converting the
break-in into a break-out. Apparently inexhaustible numbers

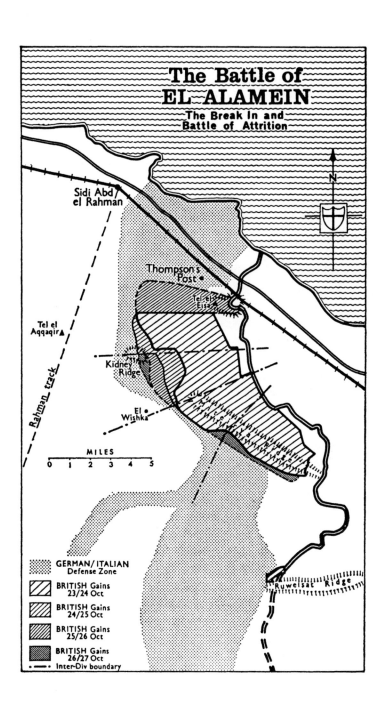

The Battle of
EL ALAMEIN

The Break In and
Battle of Attrition

N

Sidi Abd
el Rahman

Thompson's
Post

Tel el
Fisa

Tel el
Aqqaqir

Kidney
Ridge

Rahman track

El
Wishka

MILES
0 1 2 3 4 5

Ruweisat Ridge

GERMAN/ITALIAN
Defense Zone

BRITISH Gains
23/24 Oct

BRITISH Gains
24/25 Oct

BRITISH Gains
25/26 Oct

BRITISH Gains
26/27 Oct
Inter-Div boundary

of mines covered by apparently invisible antitank guns and dug-in tanks had effectively sealed the exits to Eighth Army's hard-won corridors. The British tanks could stay inside and destroy when they were attacked, but they could not force their way out.

The mines in conjunction with the antitank guns were proving as effective a deterrent to a breakthrough by the tank mass as barbed wire and machine guns had to the infantry mass of 1914–18. The Panzerarmee's main defensive gun line was still ominously in its original position astride the line of the Rahman track in spite of the hammering it had received from the airplanes and the artillery.

There was also the question of casualties. Eighth Army had by this time incurred more than 6,000—not excessive for a battle of this type and scale—but most of these were in XXX Corps, the best of the infantry; the 51st Highland Division being hardest hit with more than 2,000.[2] The tally was not excessive in the circumstances, but it was a factor that had to be closely watched, as the South Africans and New Zealanders had very few replacements available.

British tank losses had been high but the enemy's had been proportionately higher, and with at least 800 effective runners Montgomery had no cause for anxiety on this score.

The other factor that Montgomery had to consider was fatigue. Most of the units of XXX and X Corps had been fighting continuously for three days and nights and were exhausted, not to say depressed. For this is the numb and gray time of a battle when the irresistible force, weary and sleepless, begins to suspect that the object ahead may be indeed immovable.

Montgomery knew this and realized that these divisions would need to be rested before being asked for another major effort. It was axiomatic with him to send troops into battle fresh, and this was well in his mind while he pondered in his house trailer. Some kind of rest would have to be contrived for those who were to participate in the new project forming in his mind.

Montgomery emerged from his retreat with his mind made up in principle. He would consider Operation LIGHT-FOOT at an end and would issue orders to XXX Corps to secure the front where it was and make its lines safe against attack from any quarter. He would launch a new offensive with a fresh battle group to be formed by withdrawing certain divisions for a rest and then regrouping them along with others that had so far been little used. This decisive attack would probably be made in the northern part of the XXX Corps sector to exploit the recent success of the 9th Australian Division.

As the rest and regrouping would take time it must be put in hand at once. That night the New Zealanders and their incorporated British armored brigade would be withdrawn from the front to rest and reorganize, the gap being filled by extending the frontage of the 1st South African and 4th Indian Divisions. Two nights later the 7th Armoured Division would move up from the southern sector to an assembly area east of Alamein station. Finally, 1st Armoured Division would come into reserve to join the new assault force, and certain infantry brigades would be detached from their own divisions to augment the infantry strength of the group.

The first operational move in the new offensive, which was code-named SUPERCHARGE, was to be a further attack by the full strength of the 9th Australian Division against the enemy cut off in the northern salient. This preliminary action was ordered for the night of October 28, three nights after the Australians' successful capture of Point 29.

Having set the wheels in motion, Montgomery received the later reports of the day's activity. There had been another strong attack in the Kidney Ridge area by the 15th Panzer

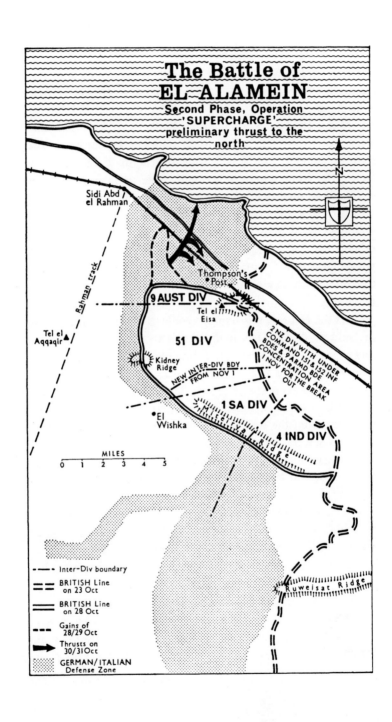

The Battle of EL-ALAMEIN
Second Phase, Operation 'SUPERCHARGE' preliminary thrust to the north

N

Sidi Abd / el Rahman

Rahman track

Thompson's Post

9 AUST DIV

Tel el Eisa

Tel el Aqqaqir

51 DIV

Kidney Ridge

2 NZ DIV WITH UNDER COMMAND 151 & 152 INF BDES & 9 ARMD BDE IN CONCENTRATION AREA 1 NOV FOR THE BREAK OUT

NEW INTER-DIV BDY FROM NOV 1

1 SA DIV

El Wishka

4 IND DIV

Inter Val Ridge

MILES
0 1 2 3 4 5

Ruweisat Ridge

- - - Inter-Div boundary

= = BRITISH Line on 23 Oct

—— BRITISH Line on 28 Oct

- - - Gains of 28/29 Oct

➤ Thrusts on 30/31 Oct

GERMAN/ITALIAN Defense Zone

and Littorio Divisions along with a battalion of Italian Bersa-glieri. The enemy formation had been disrupted at the outset by Desert Air Force bombers while it was assembling for the attack and was beaten off with more heavy losses to the German and Italian tanks. What Montgomery could not know was that Field-Marshal Rommel had watched the attack and seems to have been more impressed by the British effort than were the British themselves. Rommel, whose military reportage occasionally seems designed for an English popular newspaper, described the Panzerarmee Afrika attack in these words:

> Unfortunately, the attack gained ground very slowly. The British resisted desperately. Rivers of blood were poured out over miserable strips of land which, in normal times, not even the poorest Arab would have bothered his head about. . . .[3]

What was more important was that Rommel had felt it necessary to call up the 90th Light Division from reserve and also to order the 21st Panzer Division to move up from the southern sector even though he knew there would not be enough gasoline for them to move back again should that become necessary.

Both these divisions would be identified by Eighth Army on the northern sector in the next 48 hours. It meant that the old guard was gathering in the north. And this would have an important bearing on the new Montgomery plan that was taking shape.

But the most important news of the day for both Montgomery and Rommel was the confirmation—as comforting to the one as it was desolating to the other—that aircraft of the Royal Navy had sunk the large tanker *Proserpina* with torpedoes outside Tobruk harbor.[4]

That night the regrouping began, and the 2nd New Zealand Division gratefully moved back from Miteirya Ridge of abominable memory to a location a few miles back by the sea.

For a day or two the men could refresh themselves with the only two pleasures available—bathing and sleeping. For 48 hours or so they could forget the moldering corpses crawling with flies, the charred remains of burnt-out tanks, the stench of unburied dead so infinitely more nauseating in the scorching desert heat that never varied from day to day. For a few hours there would be nothing but swimming in cool water and sleeping through the cool night; away from the sight and smell of putrefying or burnt flesh and the ubiquitous litter of calcinated tank wreckage.

On the following night reconnaissance parties of 7th Armoured Division moved up to the coast to prepare for the division's move in a day or two for its share of the swimming and rest. No anxiety attached to this coming movement of armor away from the southern sector of the front. That morning Eighth Army Intelligence had positively identified 21st Panzer Division headquarters in the north. The division was on its way there if it had not already arrived.

By the afternoon of this October 27 there was no doubt. The 21st Panzer Division was reunited with the battered remnants of the 15th Panzer and 90th Light Divisions and elements of the two Italian Littorio and Ariete Divisions. Like a proud but now half-crippled prima donna, the Afrika Korps, taking the stage complete for the first time in this battle, led the way in an all-out counterattack on the British between the Australian left and Kidney Ridge.

The operation was preceded by a dive-bomber attack on the British positions, but the enemy forces were also under constant attack from the Royal Air Force. Three times within 15 minutes the 90th Light Division was bombed by formations of 18 British bombers as it was taking up deployment positions in the open just prior to the attack. Rommel describes what happened later:

Then the armour moved forward. A murderous British fire struck into our ranks and our attack was soon brought to a halt by an immensely powerful antitank defence, mainly from dug-in antitank guns and a large number of tanks. We suffered considerable losses and were obliged to withdraw.[5]

The chessboard moves of Montgomery's regrouping had to be covered by a convincing maintenance of aggression by those still in the line so that there should not be the least suspicion in the enemy camp of what was going on. Thanks to the abundant stocks of ammunition, the nights continued to tremble with the thunder and lightning of gunfire that seemed as continuous and purposeful as ever.

All the British units contributed to this, but the main burden devolved for the time being upon 1st Armoured Division, which was not only bearing the brunt of the powerful enemy counterattacks now being thrown in under the personal supervision of Rommel but also was having to initiate attacks itself.

A motorized infantry battalion of this division's Motor Brigade now performed one of the few outstanding *tours de force* by an individual unit in this battle which was mostly a rather shapeless neo-Flanders affair of masses—with massed mines and massed tanks as the new factors that Flanders had not known.

Between the Axis counterattacks of October 26 and 27, 1st Armoured Division was ordered to make a night attack aimed at breaking through in the Kidney Ridge area. The plan was for the division's motorized infantry brigade to seize relevant ground during the night of October 26 and establish a screen of antitank guns as a firm base through which the division's tanks could pass at daybreak. The 2nd Battalion (the Rifle Brigade) was one of the battalions concerned in this preliminary maneuver. The men were to lodge themselves a mile from Kidney Ridge on one of the anonymous undulations which, in this faceless limbo, counted as "important high ground."

They took their objective without too much trouble, but had the greatest difficulty in getting their antitank guns forward by first light, the main object of what they were doing. There were areas of soft sand to be crossed, and a number of vehicles failed to make the crossing. But by dawn the battalion had thirteen of its sixteen 6-pounders in position and six more of a Royal Artillery battery attached for the operation.

As soon as it was light enough the men discovered they were close to an Italian tank lager, with a German lager also discernible a little farther away. Early in the day both tank groups moved and the Rifle Brigade quickly knocked out 14 enemy tanks. The 1st Armoured Division tanks now began to advance in accordance with the main plan and the Rifle Brigade scored further successes with its antitank guns at intervals during the morning against German and Italian tanks advancing to tackle the British armor.

The climax came in the afternoon when the men of the Rifle Brigade found themselves (though they could not know this) in the path of Rommel's big counterattack of October 27. They continued to score hits on successive waves of tanks crossing their front to join the main battle—or advancing on them to put their troublesome guns out of action. They were an important element of the "immensely powerful antitank defence" of which Rommel spoke in his reference to this battle already quoted.

In armored warfare, as in air combat, it is difficult to establish exactly who is to be credited with how many kills, as an enemy may be engaged from several directions at once by different tanks and guns, and all will tend to say they scored the vital hit. The Rifle Brigade's claim was so remarkable that an inquiry commission examined it after the battle, taking evidence and inspecting the battlefield, making due allowance for wreckage that by then would have been removed. The commission officially credited the battalion with 37 tanks or self-propelled guns knocked out, 27 of which were still incontrovertibly there on the ground.

This was an astonishing performance.[6] But its importance lay not in the impressive score. Nor even in the Victoria Cross this action earned for the Rifle Brigade's commander, Lieut.-Colonel Victor Turner. The importance lay in the fact that this antitank screen to help the tanks forward was precisely the device on which Eighth Army's tanks had so often come to grief in the past. Rommel it was who had taught the lesson. Now it was clear that the lesson had been learnt.

There was something else. The battle showed the infantry antitank gunner that with the new 6-pounder gun (as opposed to the 2-pounder "pop-gun" of the past) he was now armed with a killer. Crews with the nerve and discipline to hold their fire until the tank was close enough need no longer tremble as the monstrous machine bore down on them. It was the turn of the Axis tank crews to feel naked and helpless.

These were the considerations that gave true significance to the Rifle Brigade's gallant action on the briefly important bit of anonymous sand which, as it had no name, they knew only by its code-name of "Snipe."

This was a symbolic action in its reflection of how times had changed in the desert. It was a kind of watershed in the battle psychology of the Eighth Army.

Early the next morning, October 28, Montgomery gave orders that the Kidney Ridge sector would go on the defensive and that 1st Armoured Division was to be withdrawn to rest and reorganize with the other formations that were already doing this. In these last days it had taken, as well as handed out, crippling punishment; especially its 24th Armoured Brigade, which had started the battle under 10th Armoured Division but had moved over on the second day to join 1st Armoured. This brigade's bleak reward was to be told that it would now be disbanded and its tanks handed over to the division's other armoured brigade, the 2nd, to replace losses.

That night the 9th Australian Division would start its attack in the north and this would be the prelude to the last act, Operation SUPERCHARGE.

QUALMS IN LONDON

9 WHILE THE formations withdrawn from the line were preparing for SUPERCHARGE and Montgomery was awaiting, without any outward show of anxiety, the development of the new Australian initiative in the north, there was something like consternation in London. "Watching a battle from a distance," General Brooke had written in his diary a day or two before, "is far worse than being mixed up in the middle of it and absorbed by running it. . . ."[1] It is unlikely that he was ever more conscious of this than throughout the day of October 29.

Word had reached the Prime Minister that the offensive had bogged down and that Montgomery was withdrawing divisions from the line. It seemed painfully reminiscent of previous desert offensives. The reaction was explosive and most of it fell on the long-suffering shoulders of the Chief of the Imperial General Staff, General Brooke.

Early on October 29, while he was still in bed, Brooke was handed the draft of a sharp telegram which the Prime Minister proposed to send to Alexander. This was followed by a stormy meeting in the Prime Minister's office at which Brooke was angrily quizzed about the way things were going. What, the Prime Minister wanted to know, was Montgomery doing, "allowing the battle to peter out. . . . He had done nothing now for the last three days, and now he was withdrawing troops from the front. Why had he told us he would be through in seven days if all he intended to do was to fight a half-hearted battle?"[2]

At a meeting later in the morning of the Chiefs of Staff and members of the Cabinet, Brooke found himself defending Alexander and Montgomery against suggestions that they were showing too little offensive spirit. He interpreted their actions as a military man. He stressed the significance of the continuous counterattacks that had been successfully frustrated with heavy losses to the enemy. In regard to Montgomery's having withdrawn formations from the line he pointed out with cold severity that it was the first duty of a commander in the offensive to keep creating new reserves with which to renew the momentum of the attack. This, he presumed, was what was happening now and he had complete confidence in the outcome.

Fortunately, Brooke was supported in his views by Field-Marshal Smuts, whose wise "elder statesman" counsels always carried great weight with Prime Minister Churchill. Reason prevailed. The rude telegram was never sent; instead, a message of encouragement and reaffirmation of confidence was substituted.

Eighth Army Headquarters was not unaware of the mood in London. While the battle was being stormily debated at these London meetings, Richard Casey, the Minister of State for the Middle East, visited Eighth Army. Montgomery and his staff were not deceived as to the purpose of the visit, and Casey's reception was far from warm. In his *Memoirs* Montgomery deals breezily with the visit:

It was fairly clear to me that there had been consternation in Whitehall when I began to draw divisions into reserve. . . .

Casey had been sent up to find out what was going on. . . . I told him all about my plans and that I was certain of success; and de Guingand spoke to him very bluntly and told him to tell Whitehall not to bellyache.[3]

But the pay-off to the story of this difficult day was supplied by Brooke. Before he went to bed he confided to his diary that he too had his private doubts and anxieties about the situation. He had managed to conceal them from Churchill and the others while he had been explaining what he *thought* Montgomery's actions and intentions must be: "But there was just that possibility that I was wrong and that Monty was beat."[4]

In retrospect it can be seen that this was the day in which the battle of Alamein underwent its supreme crisis of anxiety. When this has been grasped, the actions and feelings of the principals concerned are easy to understand. Nothing less than the future of the British Commonwealth of Nations was at stake. It was a fearful responsibility that now rested on two men, Prime Minister Churchill and Montgomery. In the circumstances and from gloomy previous experience it was not unreasonable of Churchill to express anxiety. Montgomery, on the spot, was not unreasonable in being irritated by it. It was a day of days when edginess was entirely excusable. And it is gratifying, as well as indicative of the scarcely bearable strain on all principally concerned, that Brooke could record at the end of it a happy late-night session with the Prime Minister after the storms of an interminable day: a day which inspired this unemotional tight-lipped man to his famous tribute:

He is the most difficult man I have ever served, but thank God for having given me the opportunity of trying to serve such a man in a crisis such as the one this country is going through.[5]

If at this critical stage of the battle the British could not conceal their anxiety—and there were those in the higher echelons of Eighth Army itself who did not share their commander's supreme confidence—Field-Marshal Rommel was being torn by acute and extreme anguish as he adjusted himself to what in his heart he knew to be inevitable.

On October 28 he wrote to his wife:

Today there is still a chance. . . . Perhaps we will still manage to be able to stick it out, in spite of all that's against us—but it may go wrong and that would have very grave consequences for the whole course of the war.[6]

The chances of "sticking it out" seemed even fainter when they brought him the news that the tanker *Louisiana*, sent in replacement of the torpedoed *Proserpina*, had suffered the same fate outside Tobruk harbor that morning.

At the end of a sleepless night mostly spent "pacing up and down" considering the possibilities, he was still determined to make "one more attempt, by the tenacity and stubbornness of our defence, to persuade the enemy to call off his attack," the negative victory that was the most that he could hope for now. But during the morning, by which time he would know how the Australian night attack of October 28 was faring, he had decided that if British pressure became too strong he would withdraw to a line running south from Fuka, 60 miles back. That day he wrote to his wife:

The situation continues very grave. By the time this letter arrives, it will have been decided whether we can hold on or not. I haven't much hope left.

At night I lie with my eyes wide open, unable to sleep, for the load on my shoulders. . . .[7]

Rommel reacted strongly to the Australian attack, correctly guessing that this was the prelude to Montgomery's knockout offensive, and guessing that this would be delivered along the axis of the coast road—as indeed at this time Montgomery intended. Rommel accordingly mustered his 90th

Light Division near Sidi Abd el Rahman to resist a break-through along the road, and denuded the rest of the front of German formations, bringing them all north to strengthen his garrison in the now vulnerable coastal sector. During the morning he ordered the 90th Light and 21st Panzer Divisions to make powerful counterattacks on the new Australian salient to try and rescue the battalions endangered by it. But now came news which led to a dramatic change of plan on the British side.

Brigadier E. T. Williams, the Oxford don who was Mont-gomery's chief Intelligence officer, brought Montgomery con-firmation that all three subformations of 90th Light Division had been identified in the current battle and the further news that the sandwiching of Italian and German units appeared to be at an end—the Germans were now regrouped in the north, evidently in anticipation of a British breakthrough attempt along the road.[8]

Montgomery accordingly decided to switch the axis of SUPERCHARGE from the coast road to further south where it would strike at the junction of the now separate German and Italian sectors of the line but would fall mainly on the Italians. In fact the point of strike would be just a little north of the original northern corridor driven through the minefields by XXX Corps. SUPERCHARGE would be launched on the night of October 31. (As this involved some further regrouping, the date was later postponed a day to the night of No-vember 1.)

In the meantime it was essential that Rommel should con-tinue to think that he had guessed right; that the northern attack was the start of the climactic effort, and that Mont-gomery would now drive west along the road as soon as he had created the opening. There was only one way to encourage Rommel in this belief. The Australians would have to maintain their onslaught on the northern pockets until SUPERCHARGE unloosed its fury at what it was hoped would by then be an unexpected part of the line.

It was a thankless task and a great tribute to the fighting capability of General Morshead's 9th Australian Division, for this was no diversion that they were being asked to create. They would have to keep making heavily supported attacks against the partly encircled enemy coastal pockets, drawing on to themselves the full counterattack power of Rommel's best divisions. This was still the prelude to the finale, but the prelude would have to last a few more bars than had originally been intended, and it would have to be so convincing as to be barely distinguishable from the finale itself. This was the task of the Australians and they were to resume their offensive operations on the following night, October 30.

Montgomery's tactics at this stage could be likened to those of a tennis player who pins his opponent down by a series of hard drives to the far corner of the right-hand court prior to making the winning smash into the far left.

THE KNOCKOUT

10 THE OBJECTIVE of SUPERCHARGE, intended to be the decisive break-out action of the battle, was the powerful antitank screen astride the Rahman track and the related Tel el Aqqaqir ridge just west of it. The track was the baseline of the enemy defense system and its main lateral communications link anchored to Sidi Abd el Rahman on the coast road. The track was the steel wall, Aqqaqir the citadel at the far end of the original five-mile belt of mines and defense works through which the men and tanks of the Eighth Army had been battering their way for a week and two days.

In principle the plan for the new attack was similar to that for Operation LIGHTFOOT. General Leese's XXX Corps was to start it with an infantry night attack closely followed by tanks which would then exploit beyond the infantry objective before dawn and create the opening through which General Lumsden's X Corps would pour its 1st and 10th Armoured Divisions in what was intended to be the final stampede into the open.

Leese's attack was entrusted to General Freyberg's 2nd New Zealand Division specially augmented for the occasion by two British infantry brigades in addition to the British 9th Armoured Brigade which had been attached to it throughout the battle. The additional infantry were the Durham brigade from the 50th Division and a Highland brigade from the 51st Division. These two brigades were to carry out the attack on a 4,000-yard front to a depth of 6,000 yards, bringing them just short of the Rahman track.

A this point the 9th Armoured Brigade, following close behind, would pass through the infantry bridgehead and carry on for another 2,000 yards, which would take them through the antitank screen before dawn. Behind them would be X Corps led by 1st Armoured Division (2nd and 8th Armoured Brigades), so that if all went according to plan there would be three armored brigades out in the open by daylight.

There were two embellishments to this plan. The Maori battalion of the New Zealand Division was to act as right flank guard to the main attack by capturing a strongpoint on the right of the thrust line and then taking up a position facing north while another reserve formation did the same on the left of the main attack. Secondly, at dawn X Corps was to send two armored car regiments out of the newly-won salient on a probing foray around the German defenses to reconnoiter and harass the enemy rear.

The infantry attack would be supported by tanks of the 23rd Armoured Brigade and a creeping barrage by 192 guns; while an additional 168 guns would fire concentrations on known or suspected enemy positions on the line of advance. For the continuation of the attack by 9th Armoured Brigade the same guns would provide a barrage to precede the tanks through the antitank screen.

Montgomery had chosen General Freyberg to take charge of this first phase of SUPERCHARGE because he considered Freyberg the most thrustful and aggressive of the divisional commanders. The New Zealander, a veteran of Gallipoli and the Somme as well as Crete, Greece and the desert, was one of the few men who had held active field command in both world wars. A huge, handsome man of legendary courage—holder of the Victoria Cross as well as the D.S.O. with three bars, Freyberg was not the subtlest of generals, but he was a rousing battle leader who kept his own division (and anyone else's that happened to be near him) on its toes.

In his operation order for SUPERCHARGE Montgomery had included the following sentences:

This operation if successful will result in the complete disintegration of the enemy and will lead to his final destruction.

It will therefore be successful.

Determined leadership will be vital; complete faith in the plan, and its success, will be vital; there must be no doubters; risks must be accepted freely; there must be no "bellyaching."[1]

Freyberg was the natural embodiment of the qualities implied by these soldierly injunctions, and it was the measure of his favor with Montgomery that when, on the night of October 30, he asked for a postponement of 24 hours because the necessary movement and organization of his "guest" brigades from other divisions was proving more difficult than anticipated, he got it.

SUPERCHARGE was accordingly retimed for the following night; or, more precisely, for 0105 hours in the early morning of Tuesday, November 2. The lateness of H-hour was dictated by the fact that the moon was now well on the wane.

Meanwhile during this night (October 30) the Australians addressed themselves to their allotted task of drawing the center of gravity of the fighting to the far north of the front by continuing their seaward thrust started two nights earlier. They came up against stubborn opposition and the usual closely defended minefields but in spite of heavy losses (one battalion was reduced to a single officer and only 84 men) they managed to establish themselves across the road and railway, where they were joined by a regiment of tanks. Two German battalions were now almost completely cut off with only a narrow coastal strip linking them with the main army.

Rommel reacted strongly, ordering a heavy counterattack by 90th Light and 21st Panzer Divisions on the new Australian gains. The attack went in on the afternoon of October 31, preceded by Stuka dive bombers and supported by all the artillery that could be brought to bear on the area. Although this attack was blocked with heavy casualties on both sides, it achieved for a time a limited success that enabled most of the Germans who had been cut off to extricate themselves.

Viewing the scene next morning from an adjacent height, Rommel noted between 30 and 40 burnt-out British tanks and a Red Cross flag amid the wreckage, witness to the violence of the battle on the day before, commenting: "The British were obviously getting their wounded out, and our artillery had accordingly ceased fire."[2] He ordered the same two divisions to continue to counterattack the salient.

This was what Montgomery had planned for. It meant that important elements of Rommel's reserves were being drawn into costly action in the wrong place a few hours before SUPERCHARGE. More important, it looked as though Rommel still thought the road in the north was where the big attack was going to come.

During November 1, a number of messages were sent and received which supply their own comment on the mounting tension as the battle shuddered to its climax and the two tired armies braced themselves for the last act.

Churchill received from Alexander a statement of Eighth Army's casualties in the first eight days of the battle.[3] The number of killed, wounded and missing was: officers, 695; other ranks, 9,345. The formations that had suffered the heaviest losses were the 51st Highland Division and the 9th Australian Division, with approximately 2,000 each; though the 10th Armoured Division had lost 1,430, which is unusually heavy for armor.

Rommel, ruefully conscious that his tank strength had been reduced to 90 German and 140 Italian tanks compared with Eighth Army's 800, found little comfort in a message from Marshal Ugo Cavallero his nominal commander-in-chief in Rome:

> The Duce authorizes me to convey to you his deep appreciation of the successful counterattack led personally by you. The Duce also conveys to you his complete confidence that the battle now in progress will be brought to a successful conclusion under your command.[4]

This prompted a wistful reflection:

> It is sometimes a misfortune to enjoy a certain military reputation. One knows one's own limits, but other people expect miracles and set down a defeat to deliberate cussedness.[5]

In the nightly letter home, he unburdened himself as usual to his wife:

> A week of very, very hard fighting. It was often doubtful whether we'd be able to hold out. Yet we did manage it each time, although with sad losses.[6]

The new operation opened well. At 0105 hours, the earliest time from which the diminishing moon could be of any help, the two assault brigades started their advance behind a creeping barrage. Although the barrage could not prevent effective opposition to the advance almost from the start, steady progress was made. The Highlanders on the left reached the final objective, 6,000 yards away, on time at 0345.

The Durhams on the right took rather longer, having a more difficult passage, but they were there half an hour later. Both battalions charged with launching the flank protection attacks had completed, very soon afterward, the tasks allotted them on the right and left of the main attack. The Maori battalion on the right had done particularly well. Perhaps put on their mettle by virtue of being the only New Zealand infantry as yet involved in this 2nd New Zealand Division undertaking, they had completed a difficult assault while being led by a captain—their senior surviving officer—having lost 33 killed and 75 wounded and having captured 350 prisoners.

It was a good start and at 0530 Freyberg reported that the infantry bridgehead was secure. The way was clear for the intended trump card of the plan—the shock assault by 9th Armoured Brigade on the Tel el Aqqaqir ridge, smashing through the Rahman track and its gun screen on the way. This was the difficult—and highly unorthodox—task of Brigadier John Currie's 9th Armoured Brigade.[7]

Currie's brigade had been operating as the armored third of 2nd New Zealand Division from the beginning of El Alamein and had taken a full share of the New Zealanders' hard and costly fighting on Miteirya Ridge in the first day or two. But this was nothing compared with what lay ahead of them now. Montgomery attached tremendous importance to this attack on the Aqqaqir bastion (via the Rahman track guns) and believed that, if successful, it could end the battle. With this in view Currie's brigade had been brought up to a strength of 72 "heavies" (Shermans and Grants) and 49 cruisers (Crusaders): 121 tanks in all.

At his final conference before SUPERCHARGE, Montgomery stressed the importance of what Currie had to do and told Freyberg that he was prepared to accept 100 per cent casualties if the brigade succeeded in breaking the iron entrance to what he was convinced was Rommel's last defense.

Freyberg passed this on to Currie, who in turn confided it to his regimental and squadron commanders but with instructions that it should go no further down. Not all soldiers can be entrusted with the knowledge that 100 per cent casualties are acceptable. It was with this daunting thought in their minds that the senior officers of the three regiments of 9th Armoured Brigade formed up their columns at 2000 hours for the approach march.

During the regrouping period the brigade had been resting and refitting near Alamein station, which meant that it had a march of 11 miles to reach the new infantry front line from which it was due to go into the attack at 0545. Until the moon, such as it now was, rose at 0100 the brigade would have to move in total darkness.

The unit moved off in three regimental columns of double line ahead, and from the beginning the march was a nightmare. The activities of the previous nine days had churned the desert battlefield into a mattress of dust a foot deep and the impenetrable dust fog churned up by each tank and projected at the one behind was aggravated by a strong head wind. Tank commanders with torches floundered forward on foot, trying to guide their drivers, who were completely blinded. Signs and lamps marking mine-free lanes were obliterated; collisions could not be avoided, and more than a dozen tanks were lost on mines.

So important was the timing of the attack that risks had to be taken in order to keep the columns moving. As the brigade approached the newly won infantry bridgehead of that night it began to feel the sting of the enemy artillery fire now being directed at the infantry. This caused heavy casualties to the wheeled vehicles and further casualties to the tanks. Some of these stricken vehicles burst into flames, and this in turn attracted more artillery fire on the following tanks which were trying to work their way round the casualties.

In spite of the difficulties, including the loss en route of 17 tanks from mines and artillery fire, two of the brigade's three regiments reached the jump-off area in time to start on schedule at 0545, and, mindful of the imminence of dawn, were anxious to get off without waiting for the other regiment. But Currie, unwilling to face his task with only two-thirds of his force, asked for a half-hour postponement of H-hour to 0615 to give his third regiment time to catch up after its troubles in the minefields. General Freyberg, fretfully aware that no power on earth can postpone the dawn of a new day, consented, but with great and understandable reluctance.

The third regiment now came up and, at 0615, the opening salvo of the barrage gave the brigade, now complete, its signal to advance. The three regiments were in extended formation with 3rd Hussars on the right, Royal Wiltshire Yeomanry in the center, and Warwickshire Yeomanry on the left. In the last minutes of darkness they had clattered forward, leaning on the barrage as the infantry try to do but, because they were tanks, leaning so close as to be almost one with the curtain of shells preceding by stages in front of them.

The Aqqaqir ridge, for which the brigade was making, was a little over a mile away; the Rahman track half that distance. The leading squadrons were soon across the track and bewildered enemy soldiers began to jump out of weapon pits and gun sites, trying to give themselves up, terrified by the sudden appearance of British tanks out of the darkness. But prisoners are an embarrassment to tank crews, who can only direct them back toward the infantry lines. The tank commanders did so and passed on exhilarated. For it seemed that they had achieved complete surprise and that nothing could stop them. But the precious darkness was perceptibly running out and the morning mist of the desert fast dispersing. The fatal half-hour postponement of the attack was now to be paid for in full. As the eastern sky lightened, the British tanks, sharply silhouetted, found themselves "on the muzzles of the powerful screen of antitank guns" on the Rahman track instead of beyond it as planned.[8] A massacre of the tanks now began. Almost entire troops and squadrons began to go up in flames. Instead of being through the guns, they were right among them. The only thing they could do was to charge, and a fearful close-quarter battle now took place. The enemy guns scored their kills, but not always before the tanks had driven right into the gun lines, lurching across the barrels or trails and breaking them, machine-gunning the gun crews, or crushing them beneath their tank treads.

In a little over an hour the brigade had lost 70 tanks. With the 17 lost to mines and shelling during the night this made a total of 87. Not quite the 100 per cent loss that had haunted Currie and his squadron commanders before the attack—but all of 75 per cent, and more than 50 per cent of the officers and men who made up the tank crews. Fearful as it was, the massacre had not been wholly one-sided. The tanks had destroyed or disabled at least 35 enemy guns.

Despite its gallant immolation, 9th Armoured Brigade had failed to smash its way through to the citadel as had been hoped. But its sacrificial effort was not entirely the twentieth-century Charge of the Light Brigade that it might seem. A gap had been made in the outer skin of the enemy's final defensive core for the 2nd Armoured Brigade, which was now arriving on the scene to take over. But we can sympathize with one of the commanding officers of this brigade who, surveying the smoking and blazing shambles of tanks, and the shelling that was not only persisting but increasing, remarked that he had "never seen anything that looked less like a gap."[9]

Was the effort justified? One school, notably the two regiments that had been ready at the first zero hour, would always maintain that the half-hour postponement wrecked the operation. That with the extra time as originally planned they could have been right through to Aqqaqir while it was still dark and have achieved complete surprise. Another school, including Currie himself and Freyberg, argued that if the 1st Armoured Division had followed up more quickly it would have got through. The third school, which included General Briggs, the commander of 1st Armoured Division, considered that if the division's leading brigade had attempted to crash its way through on the heels of Currie it would have suffered the same fate, for not only would the defenders have been thoroughly alerted by then but the brigade would have been operating in broad daylight, when it was madness to charge anti-tank guns.[10]

In war it is sometimes necessary to take chances. This one did not come off. The effort was imperishably brave, and the achievement—the destruction of 35 guns and the infliction of heavy losses on the enemy forces—was not negligible. The action was awful but it was the beginning of the end: the end of an enemy who was giving nothing away and who would fight like a tiger to the last.

So it was now the turn of 1st Armoured Division with its two armored brigades, the 2nd and the 8th. The 2nd brigade had been ordered on to the Aqqaqir ridge (supposedly through the doorway created and held open by the sacrificial 9th Armoured Brigade). As soon as it attempted to do so it was heavily engaged by guns and tanks and could not get forward of the Rahman track. The door, if it was ever opened, was now securely locked and bolted again. During the morning the opposition to 1st Armoured Division increased as the Afrika Korps gathered its strenth for a supreme effort to crush Montgomery's new salient created by SUPERCHARGE.

That it had not done so sooner was due to Rommel having

spent a confused night. A British air attack had caught the Afrika Korps battle headquarters and cut his telephone link with it. He had been under the impression that Montgomery's new attack had been made in the north, and he had given orders during the night to the Afrika Korps to make preparatory moves accordingly. Even later, when he learned that 15th Panzer Division, in the line farther south, had in fact been at the receiving end of the attack (and not the Italians as Eighth Army had expected) he still believed stubbornly for a time that this attack must be subsidiary and that the main effort must be in the north. By the time Rommel had relinquished this *idée fixe* (which can be marked down as a success for Montgomery's generalship) the 1st Armoured Division was ready. The division had been able to make no progress against the Rahman track and had concentrated on finding positions from which it could engage both the guns that barred the way and the enemy tanks when they arrived on the scene.

The expected onslaught on the new British salient came at 1100 hours when the Afrika Korps made a converging attack on both sides: 21st Panzer Division from the north, 15th Panzer Division from the southwest. The two brigades of 1st Armoured Division turned outward to engage the pincers. What was to be the largest tank engagement of the battle now developed as the Afrika Korps tried everything it knew to pinch out the British salient. Once 21st Panzer broke into the British north flank, but this threat was beaten back and the German divisions were systematically worn down in a shrewdly fought static battle by Brigadier A. F. Fisher's 2nd Armoured Brigade. In its unspectacular doggedness, its methodical engagement of enemy tanks from hull-down positions on ground carefully chosen with a stalker's eye, this battle might have been a deliberate disavowal of the death-or-glory venture with which the tank day had opened. Yet it finished off the once proud Afrika Korps. By the end of the day the combined tank strength of both German panzer divisions was down to 35; while the Italians, though on paper they had nearly 100 tanks left, had nothing that could fairly be sent into battle against the British heavies which, even after the prodigal expenditure of the last few days, now outnumbered the German tanks by 20 to 1. Despite this great armored victory the Rahman track and the Aqqaqir ridge remained as impregnable at the end of the day as they had been at daylight that morning.

While the great tank battle raged about the Rahman track and Aqqaqir, and Rommel was coming closer to the moment of deciding to quit, Montgomery decided that the southern flank of his new salient was the one to exploit now. There was good reason to think this. At dawn while the 9th Armoured Brigade had been riding to doom on the Rahman track, a more modest sortie from the new salient had been made to the southwest by armored cars of the Royal Dragoons.

These cars had slipped through the Axis lines in the misty half-light of dawn while German and Italian soldiers stared at them in open-mouthed astonishment, too surprised to do anything. Pushing on toward El Daba 20 miles west they had set fire to supply dumps and transport, but, above all, they had pioneered a way round the Rahman gun screen, the obstacle that was proving so troublesome. Montgomery therefore ordered the 51st Highland Division to try the same direction and to extend the salient southwestward at last light that day. The division successfully did so without casualties and picked up 150 prisoners. The crackup seemed to be getting nearer. A hurriedly mounted attack on the Rahman track by motorized infantry during the night came to nothing. The big panzer counterattack on the salient had been defeated, but the antitank guns on the Rahman track successfully held up the British advance for a day and a night.

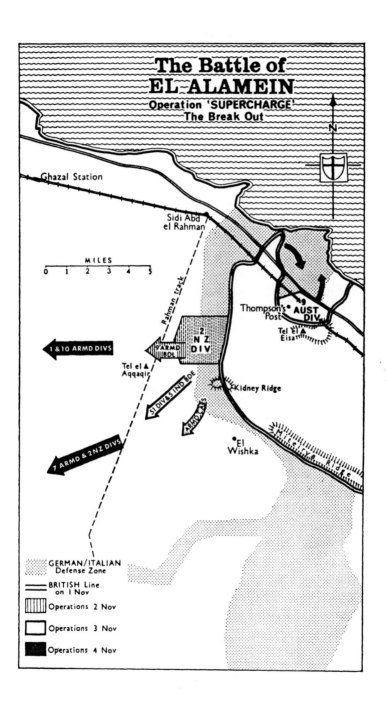

The Battle of EL-ALAMEIN
Operation 'SUPERCHARGE'
The Break Out

N

Ghazal Station

Sidi Abd
el Rahman

MILES
0 1 2 3 4 5

Rahman track

Thompson's
Post

AUST
DIV

Tel el
Eisa

2
N Z
DIV

1 & 10 ARMD DIVS

7 ARMD
BDE

Tel el
Aqqaqir

Kidney Ridge

51 DIV & 5 IND BDE

ARMD CARS

El
Wishka

Miteiriya Ridge

7 ARMD & 2 NZ DIVS

GERMAN/ITALIAN
Defense Zone

BRITISH Line
on I Nov

Operations 2 Nov

Operations 3 Nov

Operations 4 Nov

That night Rommel made the decision to withdraw to Fuka, 60 miles back, while making an intermediate stop on a line running south from El Daba. His army was so utterly worn out by eleven days of battle that he considered it incapable of offering effective resistance to the next breakthrough attempt of the British armor, which he expected the next day. He informed Hitler's headquarters of his decision and the reasons for it. Early next day, November 3, the first stage of the withdrawal to El Daba would take place.

At the same time, on the British side, a South African armored car regiment was to join the Royal Dragoons—who had broken out the day before—and keep watch for indications that a withdrawal had actually started, while doing as much damage as it could in the meantime.

It happened therefore that quite early on November 3 Montgomery knew that Rommel had started to pull out. It also happened that the 8th Armoured Brigade, trying a southwesterly attack on the Rahman track, found the track seemingly as impassable as ever. It was clear to Montgomery that the Rahman guns were going to be maintained for as long as possible as a rear-guard screen to keep the British tanks at bay while Rommel's beaten army made an orderly withdrawal to the west. There was only one way out of the difficulty: the infantry would have to pierce or turn the Rahman gun screen by a night attack. The 51st Highland Division reinforced by a brigade of the 4th Indian Division, which had so far not been heavily used in the battle, was detailed to carry out the attack that night.

In these hours of grave climax the feelings of Rommel can best be apprehended from letters to his wife. On November 2, the day of the great decisive tank battle; the day of his decision to withdraw:

Dearest Lu,
    Very heavy fighting again, not going well for us. The
enemy, with his superior strength, is slowly levering us out of
our position. That will mean the end. You can imagine how I
feel. Air raid after air raid after air raid![11]

On November 3, the day the withdrawal began:

Dearest Lu,
    The battle is going very heavily against us. We're simply
being crushed by the enemy weight. I've made an atempt to
salvage part of the army. I wonder if it will succeed. At night I
lie open-eyed, racking my brains for a way out of this plight
for my poor troops.
    We are facing very difficult days, perhaps the most diffi-
cult that a man can undergo. The dead are lucky, it's all over
for them.[12]

    It is impossible not to feel some compassion for a gallant
and skillful soldier as he faced defeat with all his guns still
firing; and disclosing, in his most private thoughts, sentiments
that must have been shared by so many of the "poor troops"
with whose plight he so closely identified himself.
    It was ironical that "the most unkindest cut of all" now
came not from Montgomery but from nearer home. At 1330
he received an order from Hitler:

To Field-Marshal Rommel,
    It is with trusting confidence in your leadership and the
courage of the German-Italian troops under your command
that the German people and I are following the heroic struggle
in Egypt. In the situation in which you find yourself there can
be no other thought but to stand fast, yield not a yard of
ground and throw every gun and every man into the battle.
Considerable air force reinforcements are being sent to C-in-C
South. The Duce and the Commando Supremo are also making
the utmost efforts to send you the means to continue the fight.
Your enemy, despite his superiority, must also be at the end of

his strength. It would not be the first time in history that a strong will has triumphed over the bigger battalions. As to your troops, you can show them no other road than that to victory or death.

Adolf Hitler[13]

There was nothing for it but to reverse his orders and tell all units to stay where they were. Later, Rommel admitted he learned to circumvent the Fuehrer's more ludicrous orders, but this was the first time Hitler had interfered with the tactical handling of the desert campaign.

During the night the Highlanders and Indians attacked the troublesome Rahman track at three points and it was the Indian brigade that made the decisive breakthrough in the early hours of November 4, at the southern end of the gun screen 5 miles south of Tel el Aqqaqir. Around this corner the armored cars, eager children of any mechanized pursuit, scampered at dawn into the open desert beyond the mines and trenches and guns, to make their exuberant mischief amid the disintegrating enemy.

The cars were followed by X Corps—regrouped for the pursuit to include all three armored divisions: 1st, 7th, and 10th—with orders to make for Ghazal and beyond. The battle was nearly over and the Eighth Army was surging forward for the kill. Nearly over but not quite. A few miles west, and still some distance from Ghazal, the spearhead ran into the old familiar antitank screen, hurriedly thrown up in a semicircle by General von Thoma's Afrika Korps, faithful to the end, and with von Thoma himself leading their last desperate stand. It required a set-piece attack by 10th Armoured Division, taking most of the day, to dispose of this obstacle. During this fighting von Thoma was taken prisoner.

It was 1530 before the enemy broke off the action. Rommel ordered a general retreat which, because of the shortage of transport, meant abandoning the Italian infantry to save the remnants of his motorized German formations, the strongest forces he had left. The Italian infantry was left to walk or surrender.

Thus, twelve hours before a further message from Hitler arrived authorizing the retreat, it was actually in progress, jamming the road westward with transport nose to tail.

The second battle of Alamein was over. Montgomery and the British Eighth Army had completely defeated Rommel's Panzerarmee Afrika and put it to flight.

PURSUIT BEGINS

11 THE BRITISH pursuit, the first impetus of which lasted from the night of November 4 to November 7, was in many ways the least satisfactory phase of El Alamein and has been much criticized.

The essence of an armored pursuit is speed and boldness to the point of foolhardiness. Montgomery's pursuit was entrusted to the X Corps which included all three armored divisions (1st, 7th, 10th) and was led by the motorized New Zealand Division with a further two armored brigades under its command. This overwhelming weight of armor (some 600 tanks) proved in the event to be something of an embarrassment of riches. The mass of tanks created a monster of administration and organization to which Eighth Army's battle-weary staff was initially unequal, and in the early stages of the pursuit traffic control in particular went to pieces. During the vital early period, when the huge armored and motorized formations were trying to extricate themselves from the battlefield and get going, there was utter chaos with the intermingled vehicles of different formations and commands inextricably tangled up in one another's tracks, mine-free lanes and allotted routes of advance.

The battle proper may be considered to have ended on the afternoon of November 4 when Rommel, without waiting for Hitler's eventual authorization, ordered a general retreat. It was not until the next morning, November 5, that the somewhat cumbersome pack got moving in its effort to intercept the retreating Panzerarmee. But instead of a bold sweep to the west across the desert, the pursuit began with a series of close wheels by all these divisions to the nearer coastal points. The 1st and 7th Armoured Divisions were ordered to make for nearby El Daba, a modest 20 miles from the battlefield, the 10th Armoured Division for El Ghazal, only another 15 miles farther on, and thence to Fuka, 60 miles from the broken front. The New Zealanders were ordered to go straight for Fuka, where the road climbed an escarpment and the retreating army was likely to be caught in a bottleneck.

But these preliminary moves were so delayed by traffic congestion or other organizational causes, and carried out so cautiously, that by the time the divisions reached the point of interception there was nothing left to intercept.

Symptomatic of the slow start was the 2nd New Zealand Division's approach to the key cut-off point of Fuka. After a start delayed and confused by traffic chaos the division allowed itself to be held up for half a day south of the place by a minefield that turned out to be a dummy, and, to complete their mortification, a dummy laid by the British in their retreat to El Alamein in June.[1]

A great many enemy stragglers were rounded up and some tank rear guards were destroyed or captured, but this was not properly the job of the formations leading the pursuit. The same cautious policy was followed on the next day, November 6. Slightly bolder was the order to 1st Armoured Division, after it took El Daba on November 5, to cut across the desert to a point west of Mersa Matruh another 80 miles farther on; but 1st Armoured's effort to achieve this was hampered by its twice running out of gasoline.

What was needed was for one armored force to have set off early on November 5 and raced straight across the desert to Sollum or even farther to cut the road before the retreating Axis army could arrive there.

This was the orthodox design for a pursuit in the desert (with its one road hugging the coast), and Montgomery's tank generals were urging just that. Their suggestion being that one of the armored divisions—it didn't matter which—be given the job and priority of gasoline supply to carry it out, even if this meant temporarily denuding the others of some of their transport and gasoline.[2]

Montgomery, however, would not agree to this, apparently declining even at this stage of a victorious enterprise to run the slightest risk of such a force finding itself out on a limb and suffering a surprise reverse when it met the fleeing Rommel, as had happened in the past checkered history of the Eighth Army.

So the powerful armored X Corps frittered away the first two nights and days making short concentric hooks to the coast. And then the Almighty showed Himself for once on the side of the small battalions—irony of ironies in this parched and arid land! On the afternoon of November 6 torrential rain fell and within a few minutes the pursuit was hopelessly bogged down in a desert transformed into a boggy morass. On the asphalt road the retreat continued but Eighth Army lost 36 precious hours. The chance of encirclement had passed. It now developed into a straight chase, with pause only for brief delaying actions, until Rommel had recovered sufficiently to make his next serious stand at Mareth, in Tunisia, 1,500 miles from El Alamein.

It was a totally unexpected but undeniably British ending to the Second Battle of El Alamein that rain should have stopped the action.

In fairness to Montgomery there is this to be said about

his handling of the early stages of the pursuit. The Eighth Army was utterly worn out physically and mentally after 13 days and nights of continuous attack against powerful and unyielding defenses. Some reaction was to be expected. The divisions called on for the pursuit had all been engaged up to the hilt in the battle to the last.

A battle on this scale does not have a clear-cut tidy end like a football game. Unless there is an entirely fresh force for the pursuit, the disengagement and extrication of forces for the new task is bound to take some time and involve a great amount of complex staff work.

Montgomery cannot be too severely blamed for refusing to take the slightest risk that might spoil what was a great victory. Moreover, he knew that in four days General Eisenhower's Anglo-American invasion army was due to land in Morocco and Algeria and that this would finally seal Rommel's fate.

It is always easy for the armchair strategist, fortified by hindsight, to say of almost any military situation that more boldness should have been shown. Boldness is indeed important. But so are knowledge and experience. It has to be remembered that on the day after El Alamein the Eighth Army and its staff were not the flexible, assured, thoroughly professional units that they later became in the sophistication bred by success and the habit of victory.

Finally, it should not be overlooked that the previous experience of both sides had shown more than once that the Western Desert was a marvelous battleground in which to retreat. Both sides had repeatedly demonstrated this. Was there any reason to suppose that Field-Marshal Rommel, so able a soldier in attack and defense, should be any less skillful when forced to address himself to the less rewarding military art of retreat?

THE SUMMING UP

12 BRITISH LOSSES at El Alamein were 13,500 killed, missing and wounded. This figure includes 2,000 missing, of whom half were subsequently presumed to have been killed. These losses were shared by the Empire contingents in the following proportions: United Kingdom 58 per cent, Australia 22 per cent, New Zealand 10 per cent, South Africa 6 per cent. The Indian division and small detachments of Fighting French and Greek volunteers accounted for the other 4 per cent.

This casualty total is not unduly high when it is remembered that Montgomery was deliberately fighting a battle of attrition against powerful fixed defenses manned by tough, seasoned troops who, three months earlier, had come close to complete victory; and when it is remembered, too, that Eighth Army was continuously attacking by day and by night. (At the same time one cannot help remembering that on the first day of the battle of the Somme in 1916, the British casualties were 60,000.)

During the thirteen days the Second Battle of El Alamein lasted, 500 British tanks were knocked out, but only 150 of them were damaged beyond repair. Tanks disabled by mines often suffered damage to their tracks and suspension only and could be repaired comparatively quickly. It gives some idea of the true picture of the tank casualties that X Corps workshops were able to put back into service 337 of the 530 disabled tanks received during the battle.

The heaviest casualties were suffered as always by the infantry. But because of the nature of the battle heavier losses than usual were incurred by the engineers, especially the large numbers employed in mine-lifting; and by tank crews as a result of the repeated penetrations they were required to make into enemy defenses whose defenders had not yet been disposed of by the infantry.

Rommel's losses are not exactly known except for the number of prisoners: 30,000, of whom 10,000 were German. The official British calculation of enemy killed and wounded was 10,000 killed and 15,000 wounded, but these figures may be rather higher than the actual losses. Tank losses of the Panzerarmee Afrika were 450 tanks left on the battlefield out of the 600 which started the battle. The Panzerarmee lost 1,000 guns destroyed or captured.

In the air the Desert Air Force, flying ten times the sorties of the German-Italian air forces, lost 97 aircraft (77 British, 20 American) as compared with 84 lost by the enemy.[1]

From the British point of view the final reckoning was not costly, for more had been achieved than the defeat and putting to flight of Rommel and his army. This battle was the turning point of the British conflict with Hitler's Germany. It was to be followed two months later at Stalingrad by a complementary turning point on the Russian front. Both were parts of the same swing of the initiative from Germany and can be considered as one. The ten weeks of Alamein-Stalingrad were the most momentous in modern history, for it was then that the tide of war turned against Nazi Germany on two related, though separated, fronts. At Alamein and Stalingrad Hitler lost the war.

The question arises whether it would have made any appreciable difference to the outcome of the battle if Rommel had been present from the start. The inclination of Rommel enthusiasts to think that it would seems to be disposed of by the fact (confirmed by General Bayerlein, who took over the Afrika Korps after von Thoma's capture) that the Panzerarmee defense plan for Alamein was devised and put in hand by Rommel himself before he departed on sick leave.[2] It is difficult to see what difference he could have made in the first three days when Montgomery's first onslaught was being held by a defense stubbornly resisting in accordance with Rommel's own prescribed plan.

The point is that this was not Rommel's kind of battle. He thrived on movement and maneuver. At Alamein he was forced to plan and fight a static defensive battle alien, as has been said, to his talent and temperament.

Conversely, it *was* Montgomery's kind of battle. He had just the iron simplicity and almost mystical single-mindedness to plan and go through with a pitiless battle of attrition. He knew the limitations of his tough but as yet half-trained army and indeed has admitted that he modified his first plan after seeing what the state of training was. The plan he eventually adopted had been tailored down to the capabilities (as he saw them) of the men who would have to carry it out. Once it was started, he had the uncompromising ruthlessness to see it through on his own unwavering terms even at the two crisis points when both LIGHTFOOT and SUPERCHARGE seemed to have been blocked.

His assurance, confidence, and sheer professionalism never wavered, and his calm—and much criticized—withdrawal of key divisions at the height of the battle in order to create a new striking reserve was perhaps the time when his almost arrogant certainty of his rightness was most conspicuously demonstrated.

In the white-hot sands of El Alamein, Montgomery transmogrified the Eighth Army in thirteen days from a dilettante force of brave amateurs into an army that was at last beginning to be professional and destined to become more so as it began to surge forward on the tide of its own success.

For the British people the Second Battle of El Alamein was a turning point in a personal way. It is improbable that the housewife, queueing in the rain for her minuscule weekly meat ration, either cared or even knew what a strategic turning point might be. But she certainly knew that the victory at El Alamein had transformed the whole climate of the war.

It was the end of the interminable years of "blood, toil, tears and sweat" when the British people, sustained only by the deep coffers of their courage and humor, the friendship of America, and the indomitable leadership of Winston Churchill, had endured bombs, bereavement, deprivation, discomfort, and a succession of disasters in lonely grandeur.

This was something to celebrate, and Churchill showed a fitting as well as theatrical sense of occasion by causing the church bells to be rung from one end of the land to the other for the first time in more than three years. El Alamein was the start of a new life. It was the justification of all the deprivation and misery. It was like suddenly having money in the bank after a long period of poverty.

At the spiritual and moral level El Alamein was an expiation for a decade of tentative pacifism and feeble shrinking from reality. It was an expiation for the appeasement which was the political extension of the same popular mood and attitude. On a more practical level it was an expiation for the neglect of its army by this people between the two world wars: so that the nation that had invented the tank in the First World War entered the Second with neither a serviceable tank nor a serviceable doctrine for its use. This had to be learned the hard way from German tank generals who, ironically, had evolved their own doctrine from the teachings of British theorists.

The least interesting thing about El Alamein was the battle itself. It was a horrid muddled messy killing match—in scorching heat, choking dust, and generally in a foot of exhausting powdery sand—in which sheer courage and tenacity, backed by superior resources, wore out an enemy no less brave or tenacious.

The battle was dominated by the mine and the tank in circumstances that favored the former and could be overcome only by a prodigal expenditure of the latter.

Strategically it reaffirmed the decisive importance of sea power where overseas expeditionary forces are concerned, and secondly the overriding importance of obtaining superiority in the air before a land battle begins. The first of these had long been a basic article of faith with the British; the second had been thoroughly taught by the Germans earlier in the war, and the British were now doing the teaching and taking the lesson much further.

The battle brought to a new level of performance the rapid flexibility of massed artillery made possible by modern communications: two or three hundred guns could be switched with accuracy from one task to another in a matter of minutes. These improved artillery techniques and the improvement of army-air co-operation, (only another aspect of the same thing) exercised a vital influence on the conduct of the Allied campaigns later in the war, and it can be said that El Alamein was the important milestone in their development.

But it cannot be said that anything really new in the art of warfare emerged from El Alamein. This was in essence a First World War battle awkwardly playing itself out in the Second, and therefore of little value to those who may be academically concerned with working out tactical doctrines for the future.

Even the British, who have a renowned weakness for preparing diligently for the last war, are unlikely to see much future in desert warfare except in the most limited way (e.g. police actions on behalf of oil sheiks). In such matters as logistics, communications, troop hygiene, and vehicle performance and maintenance in extreme climatic conditions, El Alamein and the desert campaign of which it was the summation will have useful footnotes to contribute to the study of war—but they can scarcely be more than footnotes.

Military academies and colleges will no doubt hear some vigorous arguments between armored warfare specialists and others about Montgomery's employment of his tanks at El Alamein; especially the matter of using them to extend the infantry break-in instead of simply to support, consolidate and finally exploit the break. Tank purists will insist that this was an immoral use of armor. Others will point out that it worked —and may always work as long as there are abundant tanks. Others may say that the tank is an anachronism in the nuclear age.

All these matters will be of interest to military men. Nevertheless it cannot be pretended that El Alamein has much to contribute to the military thinking of the nuclear age other than to those fundamentals of military theory and practice which remain relevant to any age. In the end it is the star personalities and the context that give to the Second Battle of El Alamein its lasting interest and its peculiar fascination.

A duel between champions is a perennially engaging theme that has appealed to all peoples in all ages since Hector and Achilles fought at Troy. Montgomery and Rommel provided the most notable example in this particular war, and their rivalry was the more piquant because Rommel had established himself as a reigning champion of long standing. He had previously disposed of a succession of challengers, and though the new and unknown Montgomery had checked him at Alam el Halfa, this was not quite the same thing as attacking and defeating him.

The British public, hard-pressed and disillusioned about the desert war as it was, could not help looking forward to the decisive encounter between the two commanders with a certain relish as well as apprehension, almost as though it were a sporting event. While dreading the possibility of Montgomery's losing, the public was more than ready to applaud Rommel as a gallant loser provided, of course, that loser he proved to be.

Temperamentally the British have no talent for hating people, so their war psychology leads them naturally in times of grave anxiety to the sublimation and comfort of the sporting analogy. Rommel, in the eyes of the British public, projected a certain undeniable glamour. Possibly this had to some extent been fostered by the news sense of the war correspondents, but it was certainly not based on nothing. Even at a distance and through newspaper reports only, he had managed to win the admiration of the British—even if this admiration was reluctant and a little fearful. After all, Churchill himself had said in the House of Commons and afterward been criticized for saying: "We have a very daring and skillful opponent against us, and, may I say across the havoc of war, a great general."[3] In the language of the newspaper sports writers it was the "match of the century." As such the British people awaited it with exhilaration and dread.

Once Rommel had obliged by assuming the role of vanquished, his lasting hold on the affections of the British was assured, for they love nothing better than a sporting and brave loser, especially if fortune seems to have stacked the cards against him. His popularity soared in defeat and when eventually he fell afoul of Hitler and committed suicide under

Gestapo pressure in 1944 his virtual canonization was inevitable. Since the war military writers of the nation that fought Rommel have more than once written in admiration of his generalship; sometimes comparing him, to his advantage, with his chief adversary and conqueror. Some of these critical appraisals are unfair because they overlook the vital difference between the tasks that each general had to perform and the different problems and circumstances affecting what each had to do. Alongside the more effusive of them should be set this assessment of Rommel by Field-Marshal Earl Alexander:

> He was a tactician of the greatest ability with a firm grasp of every detail of the employment of armour in action and very quick to seize the fleeting opportunity and the critical turning points of a mobile battle. I felt certain doubts however about his strategic ability, in particular as to whether he fully understood the importance of a sound administrative plan . . . he was liable to over-exploit immediate success without sufficient thought for the future. An example was the battle of November 1941, when, after winning a great tactical success at Sidi Rezegh, he had . . . dashed off on a raid to the Egyptian frontier which, in face of the stubborn British maintenance of the objective, led directly to the loss of his positions round Tobruk and his retreat to Agheila at the cost of 60% of his forces.[4]

By implication this professional assessment of Rommel coincidentally counters the very charges which have most often been leveled by his critics, including Rommel, against Montgomery—his alleged caution and overinsistence on administrative "tidiness."

It may be pertinent to add this comment by Montgomery himself made shortly before his duel with Rommel was renewed in 1944 on the Normandy beaches:

> Rommel is an energetic and determined commander; he has made a world of difference since he took over. He is best

at the spoiling attack; his forte is disruption. He is too impulsive for a set-piece battle. . . .[5]

What is certain is that if Rommel had survived, he would without doubt have been an honored and welcome guest at the Alamein Reunion, the largest British veterans' rally of its kind, which is held in London every October and fills the vast Albert Hall.

If a mixture of sentiment, sportsmanship, generosity, and spontaneous admiration inspired a cheer for a respected loser, the very floodgates of public acclaim and adulation burst open and enveloped the victor. The knighthood and promotion to full general which arrived at once were merely the start of a golden progress which, before the war had ended, found him Field-Marshal The Viscount Montgomery of Alamein, Knight of the Garter.

After the battle the "intensely compacted hank of steel wire"—as George Bernard Shaw later described him to Augustus John, who was painting Montgomery's portrait at the time—uncoiled to quite an extent. Montgomery was suddenly famous, a national and world personality, the military hero figure the public had been waiting for.

"It is a strange experience," he wrote in the *Memoirs*, "to find oneself famous and it would be ridiculous to deny that it was rather fun." Montgomery took fame in his stride, riding along with it. This was not inspired purely by vanity (though the observation quoted above shows that he was not above enjoying it), but by its usefulness to him as a leader. A latent sense of public relations that must have been there all the time had been awakened by events. The important thing was that he had the astuteness to recognize this and an instinctive sense of how to exploit it to the advantage of his army.

During Alamein Montgomery had decided one day to visit the front in a tank. As he was about to climb into it a soldier lent him his beret, as this is the most congenial headwear for riding in tanks. At the end of the journey Montgomery retained the beret, added his general's cap badge to the badge of the Royal Tank Regiment already adorning it, and thereafter wore no other hat—not even when there were disapproving hints from high places that this kind of carrying-on was unbecoming the dignity of an army commander. He pointed out that the black beret with two badges had quickly become a familiar trademark that enabled the troops to recognize him instantly when he moved about the battlefield, and that this was a most desirable state of affairs; the beret was worth "at least two divisions" to him, he said. The point is that without any help from a professional publicity man he had stumbled on what a later generation would describe as a brilliant "gimmick." It seemed perfectly natural now that his troops should never refer to him as anything but Monty; that they should take to their hearts this initially forbidding puritan who had turned out in the end to be such a splendid eccentric. And that they should be better soldiers for having discovered this and taken him to their hearts.

In no time at all Montgomery had become a "character." The press and the public enjoyed everything he did as much as the army. Britain had unearthed a front-page general whose every utterance and action was news. In the dawning age of the "pop" singer and "pop" art he was the first "pop" general. When he made his first reappearance in England people followed him in the street and clamored for his autograph. In the desert he was soon receiving a heavy fan mail. War-weary British housewives wrote, asking him to look after their Harry, Bill, or George. They always received a letter back from Montgomery assuring them that Harry, Bill, or George was doing fine.

He became the subject of a voluminous anthology of stories and aphorisms, most of them featuring his personal austerity and abstinence or his self-confidence. Most of them were affectionate but some were sharp. Churchill was credited with the pointed "In defeat unthinkable, in victory insufferable."

Later, his popularity with the public, coupled with his occasional *gaffes* when he chose to pronounce on political matters, reached the point when radicals feared that a Coriolanus was back from the wars, and conservatives growled plaintively that the fellow was getting above himself, and that they always had thought him a bit of a bounder.

The flair for publicity and showmanship which Montgomery developed was counterpointed by the modesty of the third star of Alamein, Alexander. This led to another of the myths of Alamein. That element in British life which decided that Montgomery was something of an upstart and an exhibitionist rationalized its prejudice by fostering a Montgomery-Alexander myth. The real brain behind Alamein, according to this myth, was Alexander. His was the mastermind which planned the whole thing behind the scenes, while Montgomery took the credit. Alexander did nothing to encourage this notion, which was silly and totally misunderstood the military setup in the Middle East. From his Middle East headquarters in Cairo, Alexander was responsible for the whole vast theater, with all its political and military commitments, of which the war in the desert, directed by the Eighth Army commander, was just one item, albeit the most important at that time.

In effect Alexander was Montgomery's impresario. The supreme chief whose function was to get Montgomery everything he wanted, to give him advice and support as required, but to leave him to run the battle without interference. And if interference was threatened, to come between his army commander and those who would interfere, no matter how exalted. This function he discharged with courage, firmness, and the impeccable tact and diplomacy for which he was rightly renowned. His outstanding qualities in these respects created the climate and conditions in which, with complete confi-

dence, Alexander was able to give the determined, independent
Montgomery his head and leave him in freedom of mind to
fight and win the battle in his own way.

El Alamein was the start of a brilliant working partnership between these two in the relationship just described. As it
was also the beginning of a new era in the relationship between
officers and other ranks in the British army—a relationship that
was inspired by Montgomery's unconventional and fresh approach, which, as time matured it, proved to be exactly right
for a citizen army; a relationship as revolutionary in its way as
that which had been inspired two centuries earlier by the
spirit of General Wolfe's *Instructions to Young Officers*.

These were the men who made the myths and the legend
of Alamein. It is too early for final assessments, but of Rommel
and Montgomery, the chief protagonists, this at least can be
said with certainty: In that private war, the war in the desert,
each brought a touch of greatness to his own predicament.

As for the context it is scarcely necessary to labor further the point that more than anything else at this time Britain
and the free world needed a victory. Montgomery provided it.
Prime Minister Churchill epitomized the event and its significance with the comment: "It may almost be said, 'Before Alamein we never had a victory. After Alamein we never had a
defeat.'"

For Britain this battle was a turning point in another way.
This was the last time the British Empire fought alone as an
entity. The battle came at the end of three years of fluctuating
fortune in which the quality and competence of those sustain-
ing the burden had more than once been in doubt. Now the
years of uncertainty were over.

At Alamein the British Army rediscovered its pride and
virtue; inspired to this end by a man who—whatever may be
the final verdict of history on some aspects of his generalship

—emerged beyond doubt as a battle commander and leader of genius.

More than any other British general of the two world wars Montgomery understood the imponderable mechanisms of morale—the factor in war which Napoleon considered to be "three-quarters of the game"—molding and manipulating it till it became an almost palpable sculpture of the spirit. This it was that, coupled with a coldly precise comprehension of the limitations as well as the potential of the citizen soldier, enabled him to revitalize the main British field army after three years of tentative and mostly inadequate performance. The driving force came from a blend of moral fervor, uncompromising military professionalism, and common human understanding. Like Field-Marshal Viscount Slim—quite different in temperament but the one other contemporary British commander with something of the same flair for leadership—he was in the last resort a soldier's soldier.

Time is bound to bring a close questioning of Montgomery's generalship; it has already started to do so, his whole nature, his every word and deed, being an open invitation to controversy. But time can do nothing to diminish his stature as a leader of men in battle, for only against the size of the crisis in his country's affairs that he was called upon to resolve can his achievement be justly measured.

He rallied his country's soldiers as Churchill had rallied its people.

ORDER OF BATTLE AT EL ALAMEIN
October 23, 1942

BRITISH EIGHTH ARMY
Commander: Lt.-Gen. B. L. Montgomery

X Corps
1st Armoured Division
10th Armoured Division

XIII Corps
7th Armoured Division (1st and 2nd Free French Brigade Groups under command)
44th Infantry Division
50th Infantry Division (1st Greek Brigade under command)

XXX Corps
51st (Highland) Infantry Division
2nd New Zealand Infantry Division (9th British Armoured Brigade under command)
9th Australian Infantry Division
4th Indian Infantry Division
1st South African Infantry Division
23rd Armoured Brigade Group

PANZERARMEE AFRIKA
(renamed GERMAN-ITALIAN PANZERARMEE,
on October 25, 1942)
Commander: Field-Marshal Erwin Rommel.
(Acting Commander General G. Stumme from September 22, 1942, to October 24, 1942. General Stumme died in action on October 24, 1942, and Rommel reassumed command.)

GERMAN ARMY

German Afrika Korps
15th Panzer Division
21st Panzer Division

90th Light Division
164th Light Division
Ramcke (Parachute) Brigade

Note 1

The German infantry divisions, though they periodically came under command of the Afrika Korps, were strictly speaking not part of it, but under the direct command of the Army Commander.

Note 2

The elite four-battalion Ramcke Brigade, though an airborne formation, was used as normal infantry.

ITALIAN ARMY

X Corps

Brescia Infantry Division
Folgore Infantry Division
Pavia Infantry Division

XX Corps

Ariete Armored Division
Littorio Armored Division
Trieste Motorized Division

XXI Corps

Trento Infantry Division
Bologna Infantry Division

NOTES

CHAPTER 1

1. It has been suggested by commentators in the U.S.A. that Suez was a British shibboleth, and that this was finally shown to be so by the events of 1956. But Suez 1956 is scarcely relevant. By that time the jet air age, the postwar up-surge of Arab nationalism, the independence of India and much else had happened to transform the former Imperial picture. In the context of 1939–41 and with the U.S.A. not yet in the war, defeat for Britain in the Middle East and loss of the oilfields must have been disastrous.

2. *The Second World War 1939–1945*, Maj.-General J. F. C. Fuller, C.B., C.B.E., D.S.O.

3. *Three Against Rommel*, Alexander Clifford.

4. Ciano Diaries.

5. *The Turn of the Tide*, Arthur Bryant; *The Desert Generals*, Correlli Barnett.

6. General Siegfried Westphal. *Journal of the Royal United Service Institution*, Vol. CV.

7. *The Tanks*, B. H. Liddell Hart.

8. *The Rommel Papers*. Edited by B. H. Liddell Hart.

9. *Ibid.*

10. *The Tanks.*

11. *The Rommel Papers.*

CHAPTER 2

1. *The Rommel Papers*. Editorial note by Lieutenant-General Fritz Bayerlein.

2. *Brazen Chariots*, R. J. Crisp.

3. This account is based on a report of the Medical Research Section, G.H.Q., Middle East Forces, July 1942, quoted in *The Tanks.*

4. *Rommel*, Desmond Young.

5. *The Rommel Papers.*
6. Bryant, *op. cit.*
7. *Auchinleck,* John Connell.
8. *Ibid.*

CHAPTER 3
1. *The Memoirs* of Field-Marshal The Viscount Montgomery of Alamein, K.G., G.C.B., D.S.O.
2. *Montgomery,* Alan Moorehead.
3. Montgomery *Memoirs.*
4. *The Memoirs* of Field-Marshal Earl Alexander of Tunis, K.G., P.C., G.C.B., O.M., G.C.M.G., C.S.I., D.S.O., M.C.
5. *Infantry Brigadier,* Maj.-General Sir Howard Kippenberger, K.B.E., C.B., D.S.O.
6. *Panzer Battles,* Maj.-Gen. F. W. von Mellenthin (trans. H. Betzler: ed. L. C. F. Turner).
7. Official *Despatch* by Field-Marshal The Viscount (later Earl) Alexander of Tunis: *The African Campaign from El Alamein to Tunis: February 1948.*
8. Alexander *Memoirs.*
9. *The Rommel Papers.*
10. *Ibid.*

CHAPTER 4
1. *The Rommel Papers.*
2. *The Tanks.*
3. *Ibid.*
4. *The Rommel Papers.*
5. *Ibid.*
6. *The Tanks.*
7. *El Alamein,* Michael Carver.
8. *The Tanks.*
9. Figures from *The Rommel Papers* and Alexander *Despatch.*
10. *The Rommel Papers.*

CHAPTER 5
1. *The Rommel Papers.*
2. Mellenthin, *op cit.*
3. *The Rommel Papers.*

CHAPTER 6
1. *El Alamein to the River Sangro,* Field-Marshal The Viscount Montgomery of Alamein.
2. Alexander *Despatch.*
3. Montgomery *Memoirs.*
4. *Ibid.*

CHAPTER 7
1. Figures based mainly on Alexander *Despatch,* with some additional detail given by Liddell Hart in *The Tanks,* Carver, *op. cit.,* and Lucas Phillips, *op. cit.*
2. *The Second World War,* Vol. IV, Winston Churchill.
3. Bryant, *op. cit.*
4. Carver, *op. cit.*
5. *The Fatal Decisions,* Lieutenant-General Fritz Bayerlein.
6. Montgomery *Memoirs.*
7. Carver, *op. cit.*
8. *Operation Victory,* Major-General Sir Francis de Guingand, K.B.E., C.B., D.S.O.; Carver, *op. cit.;* Lucas Phillips, *op. cit.*

CHAPTER 8
1. *The Rommel Papers.*
2. Carver, *op. cit.*
3. *The Rommel Papers.*
4. *Ibid.*
5. *Ibid.*
6. C. E. Lucas Phillips gives a detailed descriptive account of this action in *Alamein.*

CHAPTER 9
1. Bryant, *op. cit.*
2. *Ibid.*
3. Montgomery *Memoirs.*
4. Bryant, *op. cit.*
5. *Ibid.*
6. *The Rommel Papers.*
7. *Ibid.*
8. Alexander *Despatch.*

CHAPTER 10
1. Montgomery *Memoirs.*

2. *The Rommel Papers.*
3. Churchill, *op. cit.*
4. *The Rommel Papers.*
5. *Ibid.*
6. *Ibid.*
7. A long descriptive account of this action is given by Lucas Phillips, *op. cit.*
8. Alexander *Despatch.*
9. Lucas Phillips, *op. cit.*
10. *Ibid.*
11. *The Rommel Papers.*
12. *Ibid.*
13. *Ibid.*

CHAPTER 11
1. Carver, *op. cit.*

2. *The Tanks.*

CHAPTER 12
1. Alexander *Despatch; The Tanks;* Carver, *op. cit.;* Lucas Phillips, *op. cit.* Historians have been unable to establish authentic Axis figures. Final British official figures unavailable till British Official History has been published. The four authorities quoted are in agreement.
2. *The Rommel Papers.*
3. Churchill, Vol. IV, *op. cit.*
4. Alexander *Despatch.*
5. Address to officers, May 15, 1944, in London.

A SELECT BIBLIOGRAPHY

ALEXANDER OF TUNIS, FIELD-MARSHAL EARL. "The African Campaign from El Alamein to Tunis." London *Gazette* Supplement, 1948.
——. *Memoirs, 1940-1945.* Edited by John North. McGraw-Hill, New York, 1963.
AUCHINLECK, FIELD-MARSHAL SIR CLAUDE. "Operations in Middle East 1.11.41 to 15.8.42." London *Gazette* Supplement, 1948.
BRYANT, SIR ARTHUR. *The Turn of the Tide.* Doubleday & Co., Garden City, N. Y., 1957. A study based on the Alanbrooke diaries.
BARNETT, CORRELLI. *The Desert Generals.* Viking, New York, 1961.
BAYERLEIN, LIEUTENANT-GENERAL FRITZ. In *The Fatal Decisions.* Edited by Seymour Freidin and William Richardson. William Sloane Associates, New York, 1956.
CARVER, MICHAEL. *El Alamein.* Macmillan Co., New York, 1962.
CONNELL, JOHN. *Auchinleck.* Cassell, London, 1959.
CLIFFORD, ALEXANDER. *Three Against Rommel.* Harrap, London.
CRISP, MAJOR ROBERT. *Brazen Chariots.* W. W. Norton & Co., New York, 1960.
DE GUINGAND, MAJOR GENERAL SIR FRANCIS. *Operation Victory.* Hodder and Stoughton, London, 1947.
HARDING, FIELD-MARSHAL LORD. *Mediterranean Strategy, 1939-1945.* Cambridge Univ. Press, New York, 1960.
HORROCKS, LIEUTENANT-GENERAL SIR BRIAN. *A Full Life.* Collins, London, 1960.
KIPPENBERGER, MAJOR-GENERAL SIR HOWARD. *Infantry Brigadier.* Oxford University Press, London, 1949.
LIDDELL HART, CAPTAIN B. H. *The Tanks.* Cassell, London, 1949.
LUCAS PHILLIPS, C. E. *Alamein.* Little, Brown and Co., Boston, 1963.
MACMEEKAN, BRIGADIER G. R. "The Assault at Alamein." Extract from *Royal Engineers Journal.*
MELLENTHIN, MAJOR-GENERAL F. W. VON. *Panzer Battles: A Study of the Employment of Armor in the Second World War.* Translated by H. Betzler; edited by L. C. F. Turner. University of Oklahoma Press, Norman, Okla., 1956.

MONTGOMERY OF ALAMEIN, FIELD-MARSHAL VISCOUNT. *El Alamein to the River Sangro.*

———. *Memoirs of Field-Marshal Montgomery.* World Publishing Co., Cleveland, Ohio, 1958.

MOOREHEAD, ALAN, *African Trilogy.* Hamish Hamilton, London, 1944.

———. *Montgomery.* Hamish Hamilton, London, 1946.

ROMMEL, ERWIN. *The Rommel Papers.* Edited by Capt. B. H. Liddell Hart. Harcourt, Brace and World, Inc., New York, 1953.

TUKER, LIEUTENANT-GENERAL SIR F. I. S. *Approach to Battle.* Cassell, London, 1963.

WESTPHAL, MAJOR-GENERAL SIEGFRIED. *The German Army in the West.* Cassell, London, 1953.

———. "Notes on the Campaign in North Africa." *Journal of the Royal United Service Institution,* Vol. CV, 1960.

YOUNG, DESMOND. *Rommel.* Collins, London, 1950.

INDEX

Afrika Korps, *see* German Army *and* Panzerarmee Afrika
Agedabia, 12
Air Force, United States, 65, 78, 94
air superiority, 146
Alam Halfa, 42, 45, 51, 53, 60, 68, 78; importance of, 45, 50; battle of, 51–58
Alanbrooke, Field-Marshal Viscount, *see* Brooke, Gen. Sir Alan
Alexander, Gen. Sir Harold (later Field Marshal Earl), 33, 42, 62, 63, 100, 115, 116; relationship with General Montgomery, 152–153; background and personality of, 36
Alexandria, 4, 6, 20, 21, 45, 50
Algeria, 11
America, United States of; effect of industrial potential, 71; combined North African invasion force, 63, 141
anti-tank gun: British, 54, 55, 78, 111–113; Germany, 106, 129; 88-mm., 24, 78, 100–101
Aqqaqir, *see* Tel el Aqqaqir
armored cars, 122, 132, 136
artillery: British, 50, 54, 55, 75, 77, 82, 83, 85, 87, 101, 122, 128, 146; 'Priest' self-propelled gun, 64, 84; 'the Alamein barrage', 82, 146; German, 78, 127
Auchinleck, Gen. (later Field-

Marshal) Sir Claude, 13, 14, 19, 22, 33, 34; plans offensive, 15–16; rallies Eighth Army, 19–20; leaves Middle East, 34
Australia, 26, 39; percentage of Alamein casualties, 142
Axis, the, 14

Battle of Britain, 5
Bayerlein, Lieut. General Fritz, 24, 51, 53, 70, 144
Benghazi, 6, 10, 12, 44, 46, 65; "Benghazi handicap," 19
Bir Hacheim, 18
Bismarck, Maj.-Gen. G. von, 50
Briggs, Maj.-Gen. R., 130
Britain; special relations with Egypt, 4; percentage of Alamein casualties, 142; reaction to news of Alamein, 145
British Army; first North African offensive, 10; reputation of, 13; uniform and habits in desert, 30–31; medical services, 70; relationship between officers and other ranks, 153; morale after El Alamein, 145; *see also* Eighth Army; Western Desert Force
British Commonwealth, 3, 117
British Government impatient over start of offensive, 62–63; anxieties in Cabinet about progress of battle, 116
Brooke, General Sir Alan (later

O'Connor, Gen. Sir Richard, 10
oil, 5, 10; importance of, 4; Rommel short of, 44, 46, 52, 57, 59,
101, 102, 109; 1st Armoured Division runs out of, 139

Panzerarmee Afrika, 12, 43, 47, 52,
62, 65, 67, 92, 94, 95, 102, 103,
139; morale affected by Rommel's departure on sick leave,
65–66; "sandwiching" of German
and Italian units, 68–69; communications disrupted, 91, 131;
counterattacks by, 100–101, 107–
109, 110–111; main position intact, 106; counterattacks Australians, 124; strength, 47, 78;
casualties, 59, 94, 101, 103, 104,
143
Panzers, see under tanks
Point 29, 102, 103, 107
Point 102, 51
Proserpina, 109, 118

Qattara Depression, 21, 42, 47, 67

Rahman track, 106, 121, 122, 126–
129, 130, 131, 132, 134
Ritchie, Lieut.-Gen. N. M. (later
General Sir Neil), 14, 18, 19
Roberts, Brigadier (later Maj.-
Gen.) G. P. B., 53–56
Rommel, General (later Field
Marshal) Erwin, 11, 12, 13, 14,
15, 16, 43, 44, 47, 48, 50–51, 66,
70, 118, 125, 134–135, 141, 144:
first offensive, 12; second offensive, 16–20; promoted to Field-
Marshal, 19; methods of command, 27; becomes a legend,
31–33; illness of, 43; complains
to High Command, 43; attacks
(Battle of Alam Halfa) 46; plan
for Battle of Alam Halfa, 47–48;
loses chance of victory in Egypt,
57; goes on sick leave, 65–66;
defensive plan for battle, 67–69;
realizes importance of North Af-

rica, 70; returns to North Africa,
92–93, 102; watches Panzerarmee
attack, 109; calls up reserves,
109; deceived by Australian attack, 124, 131; decides to withdraw, 134; difficulty with Hitler
over withdrawal, 135–136; popularity with British, 148; judgments of ability, 148–150; death
of, 148
Roosevelt, President Franklin D.,
64, 84
Royal Air Force, 5, 44, 65, 71, 78,
101, 110. See also Desert Air
Force
Royal Engineers, 80; methods of
minefield clearance, 85–86, 89;
casualties, 143; see also Eighth
Army
Royal Navy, 17, 44, 79, 109
Royal Tank Corps, 24, 151
Ruweisat Ridge, 41

Semmering, Austria, 69, 71, 92
Shaw, George Bernard, 150
Sidi abd el Rahman, 119, 121
Sidi Barrani, 10
Sirte, Gulf of, 14
Slim, Field-Marshal Sir William,
154
"Snipe," 113
Sollum, 140
Stuka, 124
Stumme, Gen. Georg, 69, 78, 91;
death of, 92
Suez Canal, 2
SUPERCHARGE, 107, 114, 115, 119, 121,
123, 126, 144
Supply, problems of in desert campaigns, 8–9; Rommel's anxieties
about, 16; Rommel's problems
of, 43–44; disruption of Rommel's lines of, 59, 65

tactics, 21; in the desert, 26; British
delay in formulating for tanks,
25; for tanks, Montgomery's
changes in, 42–43, 72; Rommel's,
planned for El Alamein battle,

Lightning Source UK Ltd.
Milton Keynes UK
14 August 2009

142658UK00001BB/58/A